GO FOR THE GOAL!

TECHNIQUES AND STRATEGIES FOR THE COMPLETE SOCCER PLAYER

STUART MURRAY

A FIRESIDE BOOK
Published by Simon & Schuster Inc.
NEW YORK LONDON TORONTO SYDNEY TOKYO SINGAPORE

Book Creations Inc., Canaan, NY • Lyle Kenyon Engel, Founder

 FIRESIDE
Rockefeller Center
1230 Avenue of the Americas
New York, New York 10020

Designed by Stanley S. Drate/Folio Graphics Co. Inc.

Manufactured in the United States of America

10   9   8   7   6   5   4   3   2

Library of Congress Cataloging-in-Publication Data

Murray, Stuart.
    Go for the goal! : techniques and strategies for the complete soccer player / by Stuart Murray.
       p. cm.
    "A Fireside book."
    Includes bibliographical references.
    1. Soccer for children.   2. Soccer for children—Coaching.
I. Title.
GV944.2.M87   1994
796.334'62—dc20
94-5699
CIP

ISBN: 0-671-88232-5

To Bobby Cowell and Yuri Sielicki,
who know how to go for the goal

At the 1984 Los Angeles Olympics, soccer was the most-watched sport, filling the Rose Bowl to its 104,000 capacity on several occasions. *Courtesy the National Soccer Hall of Fame at Oneonta, New York, Inc. Ed Clough*

Women's national team captain April Heinrichs is an example of the world-class female athletes representing American soccer. *Courtesy Lanzera*

ACKNOWLEDGMENTS

A life spent in soccer has put me in debt to many people who love the game. This book is the result of that life, but it expresses only one man's way of teaching and learning soccer.

Insofar as the reader agrees with me, the book will ring true. Insofar as we differ—well, let's say that our ultimate intent is the same: to share our love of soccer with others who will share that love again in their turn.

There are many ways to teach and learn soccer, but there is only one way to play it well—that is with complete commitment to the highest values we know. Those who contributed to this book are all committed to the highest values. For whatever is good here, they are to be thanked. For whatever falls short, the responsibility is mine alone.

My sincere thanks to George Engel of Book Creations and Marc Jaffe, who helped bring this book into the world; to Andrew Caruso, president of Kwik Goal, Inc., who kindly offered advice and equipment at the very outset of my task; to Alberto Colone and Luis Emanuelli of the National Soccer Hall of Fame in Oneonta, New York, for generously opening their unmatched photo archive; to the officials of the National Professional Soccer League and the American Professional Soccer League, who also contributed photographs, as did Lanzera; and to Lolly Keys and Sean Hilferty of the American Youth Soccer Organization for their help.

Thanks to Bobby Clark, John Bramley, and Manfred Schellscheidt for their advice and to Afrim Nezaj for his old soccer magazines.

Thanks also to editors Kara Leverte of Simon & Schuster, Pamela Lappies and Elizabeth Tinsley of Book Creations, and Linda Price, each of whom worked conscientiously and professionally to transform enthusiastic writing into readable prose.

As often before, I owe another debt of gratitude to the staff of the Chatham Public Library in Chatham, New York. Also thanks to photographers Jon Van Woerden and Cynthia Greer.

And once again, photographer Michael Fredericks skillfully transformed ideas into images that for the reader will turn into ideas again.

Finally, I'm proud that despite their father's impatience, my sons, Aaron, Tim, and Jeremy, endured the lesson that demonstrating soccer for hours in front of a camera is almost all work and no play.

And thanks to all who have shared with me the love of soccer. With this book, I hope in turn to share that love again.

CONTENTS

FOREWORD

Go for the Goal! is an excellent book with which to introduce a young player or an inexperienced coach to some of the finer points of the game. The technical insights give enough of a feeling for what is required to allow people to get out and play. Soccer is not about books; it is about playing. This book will arm the young soccer player with enough background to get into action.

The best teacher of any skill is a good role model. Soccer is a natural game, and skills develop from playing the game. With youngsters I emphasize small four-versus-four and five-versus-five games. This is the best way to learn dribbling and passing skills.

From a coaching point of view, there are plenty of commonsense hints and advice in *Go for the Goal!* that an aspirant coach can use for reference.

—BOBBY CLARK
Head Coach, Men's Varsity Soccer
Dartmouth University
Hanover, New Hampshire

AUTHOR'S NOTE

Although I have made every attempt not to use gender-specific pronouns, some remain. To avoid the awkward repetition of ''he or she'' or ''his or her,'' I have used male pronouns to indicate either male or female players when necessary.

GO FOR THE GOAL!

U.S. national team midfielder John Harkes, who plays for Derby County of the English first division, scored what was officially termed the finest goal of the season in 1992.
Courtesy Lanzera

GO FOR THE GOAL!

The object of soccer is to put the ball in the goal. Nothing else is more important—not ball handling, passing, dribbling, heading, or shooting. All these skills are secondary. You're on the field to score.

With such a large goal and such a small ball, scoring should be easy. There is one problem: the other team. They have another agenda. They're trying to put the same ball in a different goal, the one you're supposed to defend.

With one ball and two teams, you can't score alone, so you have to learn all those "secondary" skills, and learn them well. However, if you think too much about passing and dribbling and trapping, you might forget the first object of the game: scoring.

If you're not thinking, "Go for the goal," you're not really playing soccer.

Play, Then Learn

At first, the best way for any young athlete to learn a sport is to play in an unorganized way. Too often in America, our young soccer players are taught that the game is about passing and teamwork and that the object is only to win games. Players drill, drill, drill, and before long soccer becomes something they "practice" but never "play." They are often told that the best way to learn soccer is to follow the training manuals of professional foreign coaches. So they drill in this system or that style, following one new manual this year, another the next.

Obviously, organized team drills are essential, but team practices and drills alone cannot make you a good soccer player. Great foreign pros were not born great, nor did they first learn the game by drilling. Instead they "played" soccer as kids, mastering the fundamentals because they loved the sport. They learned by playing in the school yard, with a lot of kids and one old ball, just the way Americans learn to run with a football or dribble a basketball. Later, they received organized team training.

By *playing* first, *practicing* later, and always thinking about the goal, they learned to be great.

U.S. international all-time scoring leader Bruce Murray goes for the goal, even when on his back. *Jon Van Woerden*

The Ball Is Your Friend

Not long ago a young Brazilian pro watched some upstate New York high school players in a scrimmage game. They were banging at the ball as soon as it came near them, effectively keeping it at midfield, safely away from the goals. Nobody made any mistakes, but nobody learned much about how to play soccer.

"Why do you kick the ball away all the time?" the Brazilian asked them later on. "The ball is your friend. You should want to keep it close to you."

When Brazilians play soccer, it's always fun. That's why they're so good. The ball is an ally, and they learn as children how to keep it near.

By contrast, if you learn soccer only by playing on a team, with coaches or parents around, the ball might never become your friend. It might even be something you want to get rid of, so you won't make a mistake with it and get yelled at.

Right?

The best way to learn soccer is to play for fun, alone or with a few friends, then pretend it's the World Cup and try to score in as few moves and passes as possible. This is the only way to become tricky with the ball. When you're not afraid of making mistakes, you will try things you've never tried before to outwit your opponents. That's how foreign kids learn soccer.

Technical ability comes by working on repetitive drills, but you must do most of this hard work alone. You can develop the finer points of field play in organized team training with coaches and teammates, but close tactics and mastering the ball are learned in solo practice and in fun small-sided games with others who also love to "play" soccer.

Remember, first of all, make the ball your friend. Then always go for the goal.

The Object of Soccer

The intent of every pass—short or long, forward or backward—should be to reach the goal as efficiently as possible. Every tackle you make is the first step in a counterattack. Every play by a defender is done with the intention of getting the ball back upfield quickly. Every midfield

Practicing against a wall or kickboard is helpful for developing shooting skills and confidence. *Michael Fredericks*

header should give your team the ball and at the same time move your teammates a step closer to a shot on goal.

However, this obsession with scoring does not mean that you should play only offensively. Nor does it mean that you should try to thump long balls into the goalmouth at every opportunity. What it means is that your soccer mind should remain open, aware that the whole point is to get the ball and your team in front of the other team's goal.

What about the defensive soccer that dominates the highest professional levels today? Should a beginning player also try to be defensive most of the time? No, and here is why. Youth soccer has nothing to do with professional soccer, but even at the professional level of play, going for the goal—or at least the threat of going for the goal—is still the driving force. Unfortunately, some professional teams don't try for the goal very often because their hidebound systems forbid their taking risks on offense. But whether playing defensively or offensively, a team with a go-for-goal attitude will execute more decisive passes, and its movement with and without the ball will be more threatening. If everyone on the team thinks about attacking the goal, teamwork will develop naturally.

The opposing team will have a tough time with such determined players. Defenders sense when attackers aren't intent on going for the goal, and that makes playing defense much easier. But when an attacker always has the goal in mind, a defender is forced to think constantly about protecting the goal, and that gives the attacker an edge. Not only does the attacker have the ball and know what he's going to do with it, but the defender is kept busy reacting to the attacker's moves rather than taking command of the situation. This, in turn, makes the defender easier to beat with a dribble.

When one team is clearly much stronger than the other, the better team's moves are confident and decisive, consistently putting the ball into scoring position. The stronger players do well in part because they

An attacker takes a quick shot in a Hawaiian youth league game. *Michael Fredericks*

are superior in attitude, not just in skill. They *know* they can score. They *expect* to score at any moment, and the ball often seems to take the lucky bounce for them. They have the right mental outlook to score and win.

Sometimes teams that are less skilled play better because they have the right attitude to win. On the other hand, teams with more skill occasionally lose because they lack a decisive attitude.

Think "Score!"

If you train and play with the idea of scoring or helping someone else score, you will see the game open up before you. You will see the entire field differently. Top players, for instance, seldom notice the faces of the

Scoring a goal is always a thrill. *Cynthia Greer*

opposition. With or without the ball in their possession, they are too busy thinking, "Score." By doing that, they are more in control of how the game develops.

Good players and good teams are always trying to find a way to put the ball in the net. After making a save, a good goalkeeper's next step is the first move in an attack at goal. When a skillful fullback takes a goal kick or receives a back pass, he is always thinking, "Attack"—not that such a player will be reckless or go forward too aggressively and get caught by a counterattack, but he will always be focusing on what can reasonably be done to move the ball toward the goal.

When a smart forward is pinned by two converging defenders and must make a quick pass to open space, he will be thinking, "In the very next move, we try to strike at goal."

While it doesn't always work out as planned, thinking like this will help you rise above those who are too busy passing back and forth to focus on the goal.

The Object of Playing Soccer

People play soccer for different reasons. Some, like Pelé, play for the thrill of "the beautiful game"; others play for the challenge, the friendships, the healthy competition, or the satisfaction of doing something well, of developing body and mind; but most of all, they play for fun. The unforgettable moments in soccer happen when technical skill and unselfish teamwork combine with the joy of playing.

Whatever your reasons for playing soccer, you'll play better if, whenever you step on the field, your first object is to put the ball in the other team's goal.

All else will follow.

2 CONDITIONING, EQUIPMENT, AND SAFETY

Soccer can be played barefoot, in sneakers, in training flats, or in expensive cleats with all the latest support and design for jumping higher and shooting harder.

No matter what kind of footwear or equipment you use, make sure that you are warmed up and well stretched out before you begin. Even a pickup game or a kick-around should begin with stretching and loosening up. Stiff muscles torn by a hard kick or a fall take a long time to heal.

Warming Up, Loosening, and Stretching

By warming up, you raise your body temperature slightly, making your muscles more flexible and elastic—and that reduces the chance of tearing. Even if you're just kicking a ball back and forth with friends, you need to warm up. Even easy kicking can pull or tear muscles and put you out of commission.

First, loosen up by running back and forth for three or four minutes—not sprinting, just jogging to get your blood circulating. When you are warmed up, do a set of jumping jacks, then stretch, very gradually.

If you really are just going to kick the ball around a little and not play hard, you can do these loosening exercises while waiting for the ball to come to you. Play it back easily and continue loosening up. Another way to warm up is by taking the ball and juggling it before pushing it back to other players. But throughout the warm-up, keep on loosening up. Do a gradual stretch with each leg, working on the backs of your thighs and your calves. Follow that by touching your toes, then doing a few moderate high kicks, with your foot going up to your outstretched hand first at chest level and working up to eye level. Finish by touching your toes again and returning to the stretch. A few sets of push-ups and sit-ups are also excellent intermediate warm-up exercises.

To prevent a twisted ankle, stretch your ankle muscles, tendons, and ligaments by standing with your feet together and rolling your ankles outward. Then, with your feet apart, pull your knees in to stretch the insides of your ankles. With your feet back together, lift your toes and so loosen your Achilles tendons. After that, stretch your feet by alternately raising your toes and heels off the ground.

Prepare Yourself to Play

Never start competitive play without fully warming up—first with jogging and light stretching, then more advanced stretching, followed by sprints and jumping for imaginary head balls.

Take a few throw-ins to loosen your arms, and make some runs, changing speeds, with a ball at your feet to help your ankles and legs. Juggling the ball through the full cycle of foot, thigh, chest, and head, then back again, is another good warm-up exercise, especially when followed by more stretching. Finally, do some long kicking, concentrating on accuracy first, power later. *Do not take hard shots on goal until you are completely ready.* Give yourself at least ten minutes to loosen up before kicking hard. You are warmed up when you begin to sweat and your leg muscles and lower back feel relaxed and loose as you high kick.

After warming up by running laps, begin to stretch slowly and loosen all of your muscles, including those of your rib cage, back, and neck. Stretching and loosening should be a gradual process, with special attention given to the backs of your legs and thighs. Mix stretching with some running and jumping into the air until you feel yourself becoming limber, then stretch some more and finish with some push-ups.

High kicking should be done only after your legs are fully warmed up and stretched by other exercises. If there's time between your warm-up and the beginning of play, don't let your muscles cool down. Wear sweats if need be.

There are lots of warm-up exercises that work well as long as they're done properly. Pay attention to how your body feels. If you take short-cuts, you will pay the price in pain and time spent on the sidelines.

Sweats Are Essential

Wear sweats during most of the warm-up to help your circulation. Take them off only when you begin to work up a sweat.

Once you're warmed up and ready, you can stay warm by putting your sweats back on until the teams take the field. Be especially careful to protect your legs from extreme changes in temperature. Whenever you stop playing hard, cover up with sweats or a blanket, and cool down gradually to prevent chills, which will cause your muscles to stiffen and contract. Even if you feel hot, you need to drape something over your shoulders and legs, and then, as you cool down, put on your sweats.

The Importance of Conditioning

Competitive soccer is no fun if you're winded, and even less fun if you're hurt. If you don't train properly, you won't be able to enjoy the game, and you're sure to spend more time injured than playing.

Your level of conditioning will vary with the level of soccer you're playing. Proper conditioning will help you gain flexibility and endurance. No matter how much ability you have with the ball, it's useless if you don't have the energy and stamina to make things happen. Your coach will develop your conditioning exercises according to your age and playing level.

Younger Players Should Play, Not Train

If you are under twelve years old, you should be limber and strong, but your endurance conditioning must not be overdone and should not spoil the fun of playing soccer. While a certain amount of running laps is necessary, it is not advisable to do wind sprints or engage in other harsh training that can injure your developing body.

At this age you should be encouraged to run freely for the ball, participating for the joy of the game more than for the competition. This is the best conditioning. You shouldn't worry too much about learning positions; the basic understanding will come naturally. If you like to run, you should do it, since that will be the best way to learn your limits.

More than anything, though, small-sided games are the best way to learn at this age.

Growing Up and Training

At fourteen, you can slowly be introduced to wind sprints and strengthening exercises, although playing the game should still be the main method of conditioning. By sixteen, however, your practices will have organized training cycles, and you will begin to understand your body's needs and limits better. Most of all, you should begin taking responsibility for your own conditioning and good health.

Your training routine will be determined by your level of competition and by your desire to improve. Developing heart and lung capacity requires distance running and sprints. Developing muscle strength comes largely from playing and practicing. Body tone for soccer requires muscles that are strong and flexible, not knotted and hard, so at this age, weight training should be included in the program only under your coach's supervision. After all, power in shooting comes more from perfect timing than from strong muscles. While strength is important, you also need to be agile and well conditioned to compete at the peak of your ability.

Conditioning for the Young Adult

Serious training must be undertaken with care and self-control. With the guidance of a coach or trainer the maturing young athlete can properly develop his body to meet the demands of every level of competition.

Certainly the old saying "No pain, no gain" pertains to soccer. From time to time you must push yourself to the outer limits. Each goal must be set a little higher than you can reach if you want to improve.

Running is the most valuable exercise for top-notch conditioning. A good sequence of interval running is as follows: Run five 10-yard sprints with fifteen seconds between each one. Take a full minute to rest, and then run five 20-yard sprints with half a minute's rest between each. After another minute's rest, run five more 20-yard sprints, giving yourself a bit less time to rest between them. Following this series, rest for more than a minute, then run five 30-yard sprints, resting almost half a minute between each.

You can work up to 50-yard and eventually 100-yard sprints, always making sure to take enough time to rest between them. To help recover when you are winded, reach up with both arms and then down to your toes. Repeat this a few times and you'll catch your breath more quickly. (You can even do this on the field in the middle of a game after an exhausting sequence of play.)

By the time you are playing at the high school varsity level, you should know your body well and respect its abilities and limitations.

Equipment and Safety

SOCCER SHOES: You can play for fun in sneakers, but to play competitively you need proper soccer shoes, which should fit snugly and are usually a half size smaller than everyday shoes.

Modern soccer shoes are made of material far more flexible and comfortable than that of old-fashioned ones, which players would soak and leave on their feet to dry to the right shape. Today, soccer shoes are comfortable from the start—perhaps deceptively comfortable, because they can still cause blisters until they are broken in.

Be sure to break in your shoes before playing competitively. Buy new shoes a month before you have to use them in competition and have them stretched a bit at the store. Put on an extra pair of socks when you first wear them, and watch for blisters. If a blister develops, go back to wearing your old ones for a while.

Protect a developing blister with a Band-Aid and a piece of coach's tape over that. Wearing a thin pair of good-quality cotton socks under your game socks can prevent a blister from getting worse.

THE BALL: Buy the best ball you can afford because it will last longer and be less likely to open at the seams or on the outer coating. Before playing with an old, unfamiliar ball, take a look at it to make sure the coating isn't breaking down, creating sharp edges that can be dangerous when you head it. If it looks questionable, either put that ball aside or be sure not to use your head.

SHIN GUARDS: Shin guards are a must in competition. Your shinbone might not break in a hard collision, but you will surely suffer the pain of bruises and bumps.

Any kick on the shin can be painful, even a routine one. If you are hurt often enough in practice because you don't wear shin guards, you might back off from a collision during a game instead of going in hard. That fear of injury will prevent you from ever being a good soccer player.

Wearing shin guards is no guarantee that your shins will always be unscathed, but you will feel more confident and comfortable on the field. When a foot whacks you hard on the shin guard and you walk away unhurt, you'll appreciate these invaluable pieces of equipment.

Shin guards are required in most scholastic, college, and amateur leagues. The ones that fit inside your shoes and have stirrups for your feet are best.

CUPS: If you are a male player, you should consider using a cup to protect your groin.

MOUTH GUARDS: Players of all ages—but young players especially—should wear mouth guards to protect their teeth.

GOALIE GEAR: If you play in the goal, you might want to wear knee and elbow pads. Gloves make it easier to block and catch the ball and reduce the pain from a hard shot. Knee-length sliding pants with padding help to protect your thighs from scrapes. For extra security some goalies wear mouth guards, and at the younger levels they sometimes wear soft helmets.

Practice Equipment

If you have access to a small goal, a kickboard, or a kick-return screen, try to use it as much as possible. A wall is also good to use. Anticipate what the ball will do as it comes off the kickboard or kick return, and master the bounce by guessing what will happen next. A ball can be trapped or played first-time—that is, without trapping it—over and over again. Work on technique with these training aids, and in a few hours you will learn more than you would in months of playing without them.

Use your imagination when practicing with small goals. Play small-sided games with no out-of-bounds. Let the ball be played around behind the goal, as in lacrosse or hockey. Play so that no one may dribble before shooting but must shoot only by first-timing the ball.

Small goals are ideal for fast-paced games that help you learn to dribble, to cut for the ball in a small area, and to give and go. Small goals also give the young player a taste for scoring.

The Playing Surface and Goals

Before you begin playing, take a look at the ground. Clear away any stones, sticks, and sharp objects. Familiarize yourself with where the ground slopes, where there are mud puddles, potholes, and even drains or manhole covers.

Check the goalposts and crossbar of each goal for stability and safety. If the goals are movable, make sure they are anchored to the ground. People have been hurt, even killed, by goalposts toppling over on them.

If you have to move a goalpost, work with caution, as a team, and make sure someone is in charge, coordinating the effort.

Common Sense

Safety and physical well-being in soccer are a matter of common sense and caution. Take responsibility for yourself and learn to avoid problems. It will make your soccer-playing experience safer and more enjoyable.

⚠ WARNING

Never climb on goal.

Goal can fall over causing serious injury or death.

Courtesy Kwik Goal

3 THE STRAIGHT-AHEAD KICK

For each situation on the soccer field there is a different type of kick—the long pass, short flick, straight shot on goal, back pass, and floater are just a few. Each kick calls for the ball to be played differently by your kicking foot, whether with your instep, the outside or inside of your foot, or sometimes your toes.

But kicking technique does not start with your kicking foot. A good kick depends first on your being on balance. Your foot's contact with the ball, your timing, and where you put the ball will all develop with practice and with playing—if you begin with correct balance. And your balance is determined by the position of your *nonkicking foot*. It is the first thing to think about when learning how to kick.

Concentrate on Your Nonkicking Foot

1. Stand behind the ball and a little to the side opposite the foot you'll kick with.

Power and accuracy come from your knee being over the ball at the moment of impact.

Keep your head down, eyes on the ball, and watch your foot strike the ball. Do not look up until the ball is on its way.

2. Take one step with your nonkicking foot toward the ball and let your kicking foot come back, ready to kick.

3. Your nonkicking foot should be alongside the ball, but not too close or too far from it, so that your kicking foot comes through naturally, ankle locked, toes down, hitting the ball with your instep (the laces of your shoe). At the moment of impact, your nonkicking foot should point at the target you're kicking toward. This might mean turning on the ball of your nonkicking foot as you kick.

4. Follow through with your kicking foot, keeping your head down and looking at where your foot contacts the ball. Let your kicking foot

swing through smoothly. Keep your body over the ball and keep the knee of your kicking leg above the ball at the moment of contact. Your kicking leg will do its job naturally if your nonkicking foot is in the right position and your eyes are on the ball.

As you kick, do not think about what your kicking foot is doing. If you do, you might find yourself off balance, stabbing for the ball, hooking or slicing as you kick, or kicking the ground. Instead, concentrate on your nonkicking foot and rise up on your toes as your kicking foot rises in its follow-through.

Most young players can kick better with one foot than the other. To improve kicking technique for both feet, force yourself to practice kicking with your weaker foot, as well.

A Natural Motion

Think about the position of your nonkicking foot as you step into the ball. Figure out how far away you should be, what feels comfortable, and what gives you the most power as you hit the ball.

If your nonkicking foot is too close to the ball, you will hit the outside of the ball and hook your kick inward. If it's too far from the ball, the kick will slice outward. If your nonkicking foot is too far back, your kicking foot will be coming up at the moment of contact and will lift the ball. If it's too far forward, the ball will be struck as your kicking foot is on its downward arc, thus keeping the ball on the ground.

All of these kicks are right for various situations, but start by teaching yourself the basic kick, hitting the ball dead center and sending it straight ahead.

Now add another movement. Point the arm of the nonkicking side of your body toward your target, and keep it pointed as you kick. Don't be stiff. Let your arm float, and then tense up as your body kicks. Your kicking foot will come up as your body folds inward at the waist after kicking, and your toes will meet your pointing fingers.

That's a good way to establish a correct straight-kicking movement. It may at first feel exaggerated in practice, but in all-out play, it often happens that the force of a kick and the movement of your body will bring your toes and fingers together in a natural follow-through.

The position of your nonkicking foot has much to do with how your kicking foot strikes the ball. Here the nonkicking foot is behind the ball, so the kicking foot will be coming up as it strikes, lifting the ball.

The nonkicking foot is alongside the ball, so the kicking foot strikes the ball while moving parallel with the surface of the ground. This gives the ball a forward rather than an upward direction.

Practice hitting the ball dead center, without any spin. If a ball spins, it should be because you made it do so intentionally, by hitting to the left or right, top or bottom, of center.

Use a Mirror

Standing in front of a full-length mirror barefoot to practice the straight-ahead kick can be very instructive. You'll be able to see the kick in its various stages and see what balance is all about.

When the nonkicking foot is ahead of the ball, the kicking foot is swinging downward at the moment of impact, thus keeping the ball low.

Rise up on your toes and lean forward while keeping your balance. Kick over and over again, rising to the toes of your nonkicking foot as your kicking foot follows through. Point your kicking foot and your opposite arm so that they touch at the end of the kick. Be sure to work with both feet.

Also try kicking without following through. This exercise strengthens the calf muscles of your nonkicking leg and develops balance.

The Follow-through

Power in kicking comes more from timing, rhythm, and follow-through than it does from strong legs. Of course, it helps to be muscular, but if your strength is wasted because of poor timing or not following through properly, you'll never develop an effective kick. The follow-through is what sends the ball on its way and puts spin on it, if that is

To lift a ball, lean back as you approach and place your nonkicking foot slightly behind and to the side of the ball . . .

. . . then slice under the ball with your kicking foot, rising on the toes of your nonkicking foot as you follow through, keeping your head down. The ball should have some backspin, which helps lift it.

what you desire. You might not realize it, but the follow-through begins the moment you bring your leg forward to kick.

As you approach the ball and step in with your nonkicking foot, let your kicking leg go back as far as it can. Your nonkicking foot should land heel first as your kicking leg reaches full backward extension. Then, as your kicking leg comes through, rock from the heel toward the ball of your nonkicking foot. Swing your kicking leg forward from your thigh, and as your knee comes over the ball, snap your lower leg forward and kick. As you connect with the ball, rise up on the toes of your nonkicking foot in a smooth motion that coordinates with your kick. Your kicking leg is now fully extended, your foot pointing in the direction of the ball's flight. Be sure to keep your head down until the ball is well on its way.

When you kick a soccer ball really well, you often leave the ground a little. Even when you are not kicking hard, the follow through motion of leaving the ground after you kick allows you to have control of the ball longer, making it do what you want as you kick, right to the very last instant of your foot's contact with it.

When you shoot first-time at a ball crossing in front of the goal, do not take a big backswing before kicking. Rather, just jab at the ball, aiming it and being sure to connect solidly. The ball's movement gives it power, and your short kick, without follow-through, gives it direction into the goal.

Know What the Ball Is Supposed to Do

As you kick, always look at the spot on the ball you want to strike, and think about where you want the ball to go. Choose what kind of spin it will have and what will happen when it gets to where you're sending it.

Is it a shot into the right corner of the goal? A long pass that should curl back and die at your center forward's feet? A high ball that will hang forever and give your teammate a chance to head it for the goal?

Never just kick the ball mindlessly, even in practice. Instead, think about where the ball is going. How high will it go? How will it hit the kickboard or kick return? How will it come back to your foot from the kick return? When passing, think about which of your teammate's feet

Soccer Hall of Famer Buff Donelli shoots at goal in the 1930s; Donelli scored four goals against Mexico in 1934 World Cup play, and later went on to become a first-rank college football coach. *Courtesy the National Soccer Hall of Fame at Oneonta, New York, Inc. John Albok*

you are aiming it toward. Think about whether you want your teammate to head the ball, take it with his chest, or control it on the ground.

Thinking as you play the ball not only gives you more control but also helps create better teamwork. You'll find yourselves all thinking together, and the unspoken magic of team play will come to life in a way that no strict discipline or forced "team style" can match.

Soccer is a creative game, and with each touch of the ball you determine the next development. There's only one ball, and everyone wants to master it.

While practicing, imagine you're in a game and make the move or the kick that will make you the master of the ball and of that moment on the field. As you learn, and as ball handling becomes second nature, you will not have to consciously *think* what to do; you will do it instinctively.

"Playing ten" is a popular European soccer game that uses a small goal and teaches first-time shooting.

Two or more field players are pitted against a goalie. Everyone starts with ten points. Each field player must juggle the ball in the air five times before being allowed to shoot and must shoot out of the air, not on the bounce.

The juggling player can also choose to send the ball, in the air, to another player, who can shoot it first-time or continue to juggle. If the ball hits the ground, the player starts again, passing off in the air or juggling it at least five times before shooting.

If the shooter misses the goal or if the goalie catches the ball in the air, the shooter replaces the goalie. Every time a goalie is scored on, a point is deducted from his ten. When a player loses all ten points, he is knocked out of the game. The winner is the last one left with points.

The goalie can catch the ball only from within a designated box, but he can come out of the box and knock the ball away from anywhere in the playing area.

A variation is to take off two points from the goalie's ten if the shooter scores with a header.

POINTS TO REMEMBER

- Keep your eyes on the ball, your head down.
- Concentrate on your nonkicking foot and place it properly alongside the ball.
- Point your nonkicking foot toward the target.
- Point the arm opposite your kicking foot toward the target.
- Hit the ball dead center to avoid spin, and follow through.
- Hit the ball on the outside or inside to make it spin, and follow through.

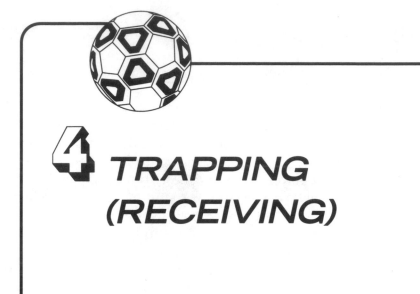

4 TRAPPING (RECEIVING)

The trap is not really a "trap," since the last thing you want is a ball stuck beneath your feet. By trapping the ball you control it in one motion, pinching it between your foot and the ground while pushing it to where you want it for your next move.

Fake First, Always

Even before you practice the simple side-foot trap, think "Fake." Faking is one of the most important moves in all soccer. Without it, everything you did would be obvious to the other team and therefore easier to stop. With it, you make the defender pause a moment, responding to the fake, before coming in to tackle.

Get in the habit of throwing a fake every time you receive the ball, even from a kick return. As the ball is coming toward you, pretend there is a defender barreling down on you and throw a hip and shoulder fake before you trap the ball. It will help you to think about your next move and give you an instant to look around.

Trapping a Ball Moving on the Ground

Done with the inside or outside of your foot, the basic trap is meant to put the ball where you want it. *However, the trap should not stop the ball dead.*

In the basic trap, make a right angle with the heels of your trapping foot and nontrapping foot, and keep your balance well forward. If the ball takes a bad bounce or you misplay it, the corner will help confine the ball and keep it out in front of you.

Always trap downward on the ball, imparting a slight backspin so that it stays close to you. Don't pin the ball hard against the ground, but be firm. Trap decisively and put the ball where you want it with one motion.

This drill and the ones that that follow are done with a partner standing ten yards away. For the basic trap, your partner will push the ball to you on the ground. (These drills can also be done alone with a kickboard, by trapping the ball as it rebounds from the board.)

THE BASIC TRAP

1. Lean forward, bent a little at your waist, and charge the moving ball. Never wait for the ball to come to you.

2. Throw a fake as you go, and when you are directly over the ball, gently and quickly squeeze it against the ground with the inside or outside of your foot.

3. Keep your balance and weight on your nontrapping foot. Do not let your trapping foot touch the ground.

4. Lift your trapping foot soon enough to trap *downward* on the ball. Always *play the ball;* never let the ball just hit your foot.

5. Make this trap with the arch or the front outside half of your foot, your toes curled up. Bring your foot down on the upper half of the ball. When using the inside of your foot, put pressure on the ball with the ball of your foot.

6. Get as much of your foot on the ball as possible in order to control it more easily.

7. Push the ball to the side with your trapping foot, staying well over the ball with your body.

8. Look up quickly to see who's around you and throw another fake.

9. After trapping the ball, keep it moving. Do not let it get back between your legs.

Remember, you're not pinning the ball against the ground. Instead, you're gently giving it backspin, which keeps it close.

Trapping a Bouncing Ball

You can take control of a high-bouncing ball by using the same basic techniques described above. The difference is that this trap requires better timing and concentration.

As the ball bounces, charge it, throw a fake, and pinch the ball against the ground with the inside or outside of your foot. Trap the ball just as it hits the ground. You have to play the ball more aggressively when it's bouncing and put your foot a little higher up on it, forcing it downward. Lean over it as you trap. Remember to curl your toes up and put spin on the ball.

Again, do not let the ball slip back between your legs. Keep it out in front or push it to one side or the other.

The trap can also be made with the sole of your foot, heel down and toes up. This often pushes the ball out in front of you, which is good when you are running forward and want to move quickly.

Of course, sole-of-the-foot trapping makes it easier for the defender to get the ball because you are not leaning over it; it is farther out in front of you and exposed.

Trapping the Ball Out of the Air

The ball should do what you want it to, so when you have to take a ball down, do it with confidence. Keep your eyes on it. Play it firmly downward while giving a little to absorb the impact and to catch it slightly.

When taking the ball out of the air, the same basic trapping principles apply: Keep your eyes on the ball, keep your weight balanced on your nontrapping leg, and keep the ball out in front of you, or wherever you want it to go.

As you take the ball down, stay up on the toes of your nontrapping foot for better balance and flexibility. Curl up the toes of your trapping foot to get more control of the ball as you take it down. If you point your toes downward, the ball will just bounce off. Feel the ball; catch it in the arch of your foot or on your instep with your toes curled up.

An excellent drill for taking a bouncing ball out of the air is to kick it up and actually catch it with your instep and curled toes. Use the backs of your toes, not your rigid instep, to control the ball.

Using Your Thigh to Control the Ball

When taking a high ball on your thigh, keep your eyes on the ball and stay on the toes of your nontrapping foot. Don't hold your thigh rigid at the point of contact with the ball. Let your thigh give a little to

When bringing the ball under control with your thigh, keep your balance forward, use your upper thigh to take the ball, and place the ball exactly where you want it in one motion.

absorb the ball's impact, and in the same movement make the ball drop exactly where you want it. Make sure it strikes your thigh, not your knee, just at the base of the large muscle, which will give you better control. Don't catch the ball too high on your leg, where the muscle is thick.

If the ball is coming at you as a line drive, catch it by giving a little with your thigh as well as with your bent nontrapping leg. As always, if you know where you want the ball to go, the actual trap will be that much easier to execute.

Chesting or Heading the Ball as a Trap

When the ball is too high for a trap with your foot or thigh, use your chest. If you back off to let the ball fall to where your thigh or foot can control it, the opponent might charge through you and get the ball first.

Keep your eyes on the ball and take it high on your chest—usually on one pectoral muscle or another and not dead center on your breast-bone. Give with your chest at the instant of contact and let the ball drop to your feet, where you want it to be.

This move is best practiced with a partner throwing or bouncing the ball to you. You should knock the ball downward as you trap it.

When chesting a ball that is bouncing or coming downward, lean back and take the ball high on your chest, giving a little to kill it.

Try changing the ball's direction as you trap with your chest. Also try driving the ball with your chest and gathering it with your feet as you sprint. Or take the ball under control with your chest and then play it with your thigh.

Heading the ball to trap it is best learned by practicing keeping the ball up. Get squarely under the ball as you juggle with your head and practice catching it on your forehead.

Generally, in a game situation, keeping the ball close after heading it is hard to do because you seldom have the time to kill the ball, drop it to your feet, and then play it. The chest works better for trapping in most cases.

Practicing Trapping

The simplest and best way to practice trapping is to kick the ball up and trap it over and over—with the outside and inside of your foot, left foot and right foot. Each time remember to throw a little fake, as if someone were challenging you for the ball. Vary the exercises by kicking off a kickboard or a kick return and then trapping the ball as it rebounds.

For practice in a game situation, plan to try not to play the ball first-time, but trap first and then play it. Do the same thing when kicking around with friends, always making a good trap before you kick the ball back.

The much-used four-corner drill is an effective way to learn good trapping under pressure (see diagram). This is also one of the best methods of learning how to move quickly to a "square" position for a pass from a teammate who is being challenged. The drill can be varied, with four players at the corners and two defenders in the middle. If need be, the square can be defined by the placement of cones at the corners and the ball should be kept within the square.

Teaching Yourself to Trap

Trapping well cannot be learned simply by playing games or kicking around. You must make a conscious decision to understand and master the skill.

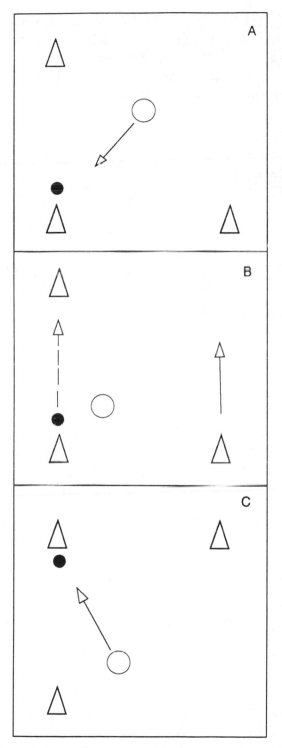

The four-corner drill: Players stand at three corners of a ten-yard square, a fourth player, the challenger, in the middle. The three players pass the ball back and forth to one another around the outside of the square, running to the unoccupied corner to receive a "square" or ninety-degree pass. If you do this drill by trapping first and then playing the ball, you will get a good sense of how quickly a defender can charge you and what it takes to trap and then pass the ball under pressure. When the defender intercepts the ball, the player who last touched it takes the defender's place in the middle.

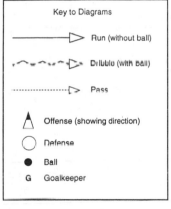

Key to Diagrams

→▷ Run (without ball)

～～▷ Dribble (with ball)

┄┄▷ Pass

△ Offense (showing direction)

○ Defense

● Ball

G Goalkeeper

As our Brazilian pro said, "The ball is your friend. Your should want to have it close to you." Make friends with the ball by teaching yourself how to trap it. Learning this has to be done alone, just you and the ball. As tedious as this can be, it is extremely rewarding when you finally take the ball under control naturally, making it look easy.

 POINTS TO REMEMBER

- Keep your eyes on the ball.
- Charge the ball, throwing a fake.
- Trap *downward* on the ball.
- Lean over the ball.
- Move the ball immediately to where you want it to be.

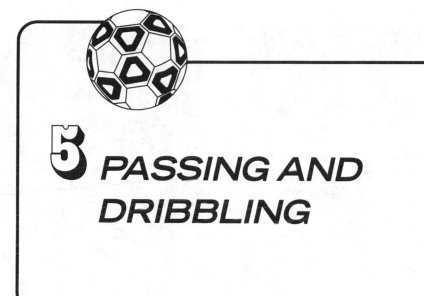

5 PASSING AND DRIBBLING

No good soccer team passes just to display good teamwork. No good soccer player dribbles just for the sake of dribbling. There has to be a purpose behind passing and dribbling, and that purpose, first and foremost, is to get someone into position to shoot on goal. By learning to pass and dribble well, you will have the necessary skills to outwit your opponent.

The Basic Pass

Pushing the ball with the inside of your foot is the fundamental pass, the simplest kick in soccer. Once again, balance is the key; you must play the ball solidly and accurately, recovering your balance quickly so that you can continue playing.

As in the straight-ahead kick, the position of your nonkicking foot determines the effectiveness of the basic pass. Your nonkicking foot is positioned beside the ball, with your center of gravity over the ball. Bring your kicking leg back a short distance, turning your knee and

The push pass is the basic kick in soccer, the object being to give your teammate an easy ball to handle. The approach is made with your shoulders square to the direction of the kick, foot turned outward, toes raised, and ankle locked.

At the moment of impact, your head is down, foot still locked, and the ball is kicked solidly, with enough speed to get it quickly to your teammate, but not making it too fast to handle.

Your kicking foot follows through, toes still curled up. Practice this kick with a partner, first-timing the ball, and after a short follow-through, pull your kicking leg back quickly so both feet are on the ground and you're back on balance, ready for the return pass.

foot perpendicular to your nonkicking foot, which is pointing in the direction of the kick. The heel of your kicking foot is down, the toes curled up, the ankle locked.

Your foot is brought forward, swinging like a pendulum, and kept stiffly perpendicular to your nonkicking foot. Strike the ball solidly with the arch of your foot, pushing it more than kicking it. Maintain contact with the ball as you push it, using your heel and curled toes to help control the direction of the ball.

This kick should first be learned with a motionless ball, and later with a moving ball kicked back and forth with a partner or two.

Once again, you decide what the ball will do as you kick it. Do not let it just roll away, but place it, impart spin to it, and above all be accurate.

The inside-of-the-foot pass, or push pass, is designed for accuracy and control. It is not meant to be a slow or weak pass, but should be struck solidly and as fast as needed in the game situation.

Variations will make the ball lift (set your nonkicking foot back and/ or hit low on the ball), curl (strike the outside of the ball), or roll with topspin (hit the top half of the ball).

In a real match, you might only use the classic inside-of-the-foot pass three or four times if you're a beginning player. However, learning how to use this pass is essential to playing a careful, controlled game. The fewer the number of players, the more often each will use this pass, so practice small-sided soccer often to learn it.

When you practice inside-of-the-foot kicking with a moving ball, concentrate on playing the ball downward until you have good control of the kick. A moving ball has force of its own, so you should strike its upper half, leaning over it and guiding it. This makes a sharp, clean, and accurate pass that is easy for your teammate to handle.

Once the timing for the push pass is developed, practice quickly pulling your kicking foot back after the pass is made. This helps to maintain balance and will counteract the tendency to fall forward. End the kick back on both feet, ready to go, and not with your kicking foot flat on the ground out in front of you.

Using a Wall, Kickboard, or Kick-Return Screen

Everyone needs to spend time practicing the fundamentals of the game and honing skills. The kickboard returns the ball according to how hard or high or slowly you kick. Therefore, there is no better way to learn what the ball and your body will do with different kicks.

When you work at a wall, kickboard, or kick return, start off by making a basic trap each time the ball comes to you, developing your ability to trap and control the ball in one motion, with one touch. Then try returning the ball with either a straight kick or a push pass.

After you've worked on the trap-and-kick combination, practice first-timing the ball, kicking as fast and as often as you can.

Always remember to use both feet in these drills. You must become skilled with both feet to play soccer well. Working with your weak leg sometimes has its surprises. For example, some players can kick a ball first-time better with their left leg than their right, even though their right is better at everything else. The kickboard, wall, or kick return will help you develop both feet effectively as long as you don't cheat and use only one foot because it's easier or more fun at first.

POINTS TO REMEMBER

- Keep your shoulders perpendicular to the target.
- Turn your kicking foot and knee perpendicular to your nonkicking foot and curl up your toes, locking your ankle.
- Strike the ball with a pendulum motion.
- Push the ball, keeping your center of gravity well over it.
- Never let your toes hang or point downward as you kick.

Juggling

Like practicing push passes against a kickboard, wall, or kick return, juggling is an excellent way to become more comfortable with the ball. From basic juggling you can learn trapping, chesting, heading, and kneeing the ball. No amount of playing can teach what an hour of juggling can.

Start juggling by dropping the ball to your foot, which is curled up a little, and kick the center of the ball, hitting it up only a few feet. With each kick, put the ball just where you want it. Lean forward a little, and keep the ball between the height of your ankle and knee.

Kick the ball straight up so that you know where it will come down. Keep your arms out for balance, relax, and let the ball come down to your foot rather than going after it.

Practice juggling the ball, keeping it up with your knee or foot, sometimes kicking it up to your head, then bringing it back to your chest.

As you get better, put the ball into play, lifting it off the ground by pulling it back with the sole of your foot and scooping or flicking it up. Let it come down and play it again, still not too hard, and always keep it just where you want it. You play the ball—it does not play you.

You can lift the ball and take it on your thigh or knee and juggle it that way as well. Juggling with your thigh teaches you to master a ball that is too high for your foot and too low for your chest or head. The height of the ball as you juggle should be your decision, not the ball's. Whack it up high, then go and get it, catching it on your thigh. Try kicking it up to your chest or your head, learning to move it from one area to the other. Do this over and over again and you'll soon be natural with the ball.

Close-Quarters Dribbling

Try this simple but demanding drill to teach yourself ball control.

With the outside of your foot kick the ball around in as small a circle as you can. You must stay over the ball, leaning forward and snapping your foot downward at the side of the ball to make it move and also give it a little backspin to keep it close. When you're turning

Practice close-quarters dribbling by turning with the ball in tight circles, chopping down with the outside or inside of your foot as you turn. Keep your center of gravity over the ball.

See how fast you can go and how tight a circle you can make while still imparting a solid chop to the ball. The ball will have backspin if played properly.

rapidly around the ball and it seems to be moving very little, you can be sure you're learning fundamental control. Do this drill with the inside of your foot, too.

Close-quarters dribbling teaches you to keep your weight over the ball, so you can keep the defender from knocking you off the ball with a tackle.

Dribbling with the Sole of Your Foot

Good ball control also involves moving the ball with the sole of your foot.

With the ball in front of you, stand comfortably, arms out, and place one foot lightly on the top of the ball. The ball of your foot, the knob just behind your big toe, should be a little ahead of the point where sole meets ball. Your other foot should be placed so that you feel completely balanced. Begin to hop backward, and at each hop pull the ball back with a light touch of your sole.

Your weight should be on your hopping foot, not on the ball. Do not let the ball get caught against your hopping foot or underneath you. As always, keep your center of gravity over the ball.

Change feet and try the same thing. Go backward in a circle or do figure eights, staying in control of the ball at all times.

Now hop forward, pushing the ball with the sole of your foot. This is much more difficult and is less likely to be used in a game, but it does teach ball control and helps develop strength in your calf muscles.

A variation on these drills is to use the arch of your foot instead of the sole to move the ball. Practicing this move, go sideways or make a full circle.

 POINTS TO REMEMBER

- Keep your center of gravity over the ball when juggling or dribbling.
- Use backspin on the ball to keep it close to you.
- Play the ball; don't let it play you.

Dribbling and Weaving

Learning to dribble well involves learning to fake and swerve and change directions. It also means making the defender react to your moves, thus staying one step ahead of him.

Set up cones (or other markers) in a line and dribble your way through them. Use one foot or the other, inside and outside, to push the ball. Don't worry at first about form or speed, but just get the feeling of moving and weaving through the cones.

As you dribble, give the ball a snap downward with the outside or inside of your foot to impart backspin. Strike the ball's lower half to do

While dribbling between cones, keep your weight over the ball, stay tight to the cones, and build up speed as your technique improves. Alternately use the outside and inside of your foot to cut around the cones.

this. Backspin keeps the ball from rolling away. Do not let the ball get more than a step ahead of you, and keep leaning forward as you run.

Try dribbling using only the outside of your foot, alternating feet as you go around the cone. Vary your speed, and pretend you're tricking a defender, rolling your shoulders from side to side to practice feinting.

Dribbling for speed is usually easier with the outside of your foot. You push the ball with backspin, using the same foot, touching it as often as possible to get a feel for the ball. (In a game, you would push

In the basic two-fake move, approach the defender with a slight hesitation and get close enough so the final move will get you and the ball through. Then, with the ball moving forward all the time, fake sharply right, then . . .

. . . fake left with your entire body—not just with your feet—so that the outside of your right foot naturally comes into position to . . .

it out and chase it, touching it as little as possible so as to get up speed for a fast breakaway dribble.)

The Two-Fake Move

With a partner as the defender, dribble toward him from about ten yards away. (If you are practicing alone, use two cones or a pair of

. . . suddenly push the ball sharply to the right, getting well past the defender, who should have his weight on the left foot. In the same motion, drive through with your body, bringing your left leg past the defender and taking the defender's charge with your left arm and shoulder.

sneakers to represent the defender's feet.) Four yards away fake right, that is, throw your shoulders and right leg to the right as if you were going to push the ball past on that side. You can also use your head to fake. On the next step, fake left in the same way, but do not touch the ball, which should be rolling just in front of you. Your weight is now on your left leg. Use this leg to power yourself past the defender.

Drive off your left leg toward the right while pushing the ball with the outside of your right foot past the defender's left leg. The ball must jump out fast and have backspin so it doesn't roll too far away, yet it needs to be out of the defender's reach.

U.S. national team star John Harkes shields the ball while dribbling past a Trinidad-Tobago player as teammate Steve Trittschuh looks on. *Jon Van Woerden*

Pushing off your right leg, spring past the defender with long-reaching strides, throwing your left leg forward to block the defender's attempt to get in your way. Get your left shoulder and left leg past him as quickly as possible, since that is the side he will try to block.

This basic two-fake dribbling move works because the defender tends to take the second fake, leaving his weight on the left foot. Momentarily caught leaning the wrong way, the defender will be a split second behind your final, passing move.

Remember, beat the defender to the side where his weight is planted. The defender's planted foot cannot be moved until his weight comes off it. If you try to beat a defender on the side where his leg is not planted, you'll find your path blocked.

Practice this drill with both feet—on both sides of the defender. If the final move is quick and you stay with the ball, this simple two-fake dribble is consistently effective even when the defender is ready for it.

POINTS TO REMEMBER

- Fake twice so that the defender commits to the second fake.
- Beat the defender to the side where his leg is planted.
- Make your passing move quick, and stay close to the ball.
- Play the ball far enough ahead so you get away from the defender.
- Put backspin on the ball so it does not run away from you.
- Follow the ball through immediately and get your left leg and shoulder past the imaginary defender.

6 HEADING

In soccer, few things are more satisfying than heading the ball well. The head ball is always taken in an exciting moment—a one-on-one battle for a high cross, a defensive clearance at the last instant, a shot on goal by a player who seems to have come from nowhere.

There are many different heading situations in a game, and the head ball can be taken in many different ways, but the basic technique of meeting the ball is always the same: *Keep your eyes on the ball and strike with the bony part of your forehead just below your hairline.*

Timing, style of jump, body angle, and force required depend on the game situation. First, however, the basic method of head meeting ball must be learned, correctly and safely.

Heading While Holding the Ball

You can teach yourself what it feels like to head the ball solidly, accurately, and confidently. The following basic drill can be done with or without a partner. You'll notice rapid improvement right from the start.

1. Stand with feet comfortably apart.

2. Hold the ball lightly a little above eye level, hands on opposite sides of the ball.

3. Lean back at your waist so that you feel the strain in your upper thighs.

4. Tuck in your chin and tighten your neck muscles.

5. With the full force of your upper body, head the ball at the same time you draw the ball back against your forehead.

6. Keep your feet on the ground and your eyes open—they'll close automatically for an instant—as you strike the ball.

7. Head the ball at dead center. Your forehead and the ball should meet directly above your chest. This is the point of maximum power. If you head the ball while leaning too far forward, you're off balance and can't get solid contact. If you head the ball while leaning too far back, then the ball is striking you rather than you striking the ball. This will result in a head ball that is weak, poorly aimed, and sometimes painful. The ball headed dead center should have no spin.

8. *Aim the ball where you want it to go.*

Variations on Heading While Holding

Do the basic heading drill outlined above against a kickboard or wall, trying to increase power as you go. You'll soon come to learn the feeling and sound of a solid head ball and recognize its power as it hits the backboard or wall.

When you're ready, put backspin on the ball by hitting it a little below center. This will lift the flight of the ball. If you strike the ball above center, it will drop. (You'll probably also hit your nose, so don't do it on purpose.)

When heading with a partner, get in the habit of starting with a hand-held ball. Remember, *hit straight through the ball toward a target.* Gradually increase the distance between you to get a feeling for how power and distance depend more on timing than on physical strength.

Try the basic heading drill while seated to better understand the movement of your upper body, which provides the power.

Also try the drill on both knees, again concentrating on the feeling of your upper body snapping forward.

In the basic heading drill, hold the ball at about eye level and lean back . . .

. . . then thrust your upper body forward and at the same instant pull the ball back, heading the ball at a point directly above your chest where you get the most power . . .

. . . and then follow through with all of your strength, your eyes on the ball.

Once you master the basic heading drill while seated or on your knees, it will be even easier standing.

Power and Accuracy

You will discover that power does not come from your neck, which should be held rigid in the straight-ahead head ball. Feel the power surge through your legs and then through your upper body like a whip. The final movement (and force) of the whip is your head's contact with the ball. For maximum power, always head right through the ball, keeping as much of your forehead in contact with the ball for as long as possible.

The power of a well-timed head ball is usually not seen in any violent movement of the soccer player, but the power is there, and it always propels the ball decisively. After practicing heading the ball out of your own hands, you'll learn how to take a head ball that comes from another player. Then you can build on this basic technique by practicing the jump.

Jumping for Head Balls

In leaping for a head ball, timing is critical—not only timing contact with the ball, but timing your jump so that when you meet the ball, you are at the peak of your jump, neither rising nor falling.

Think of the jump shot in basketball: It's best taken when the shooter is hanging momentarily in midair. The shooter has full control of his body at this point and is able to aim the shot. Leaping for a head ball is much the same.

Run, jump, arc your body back, and hang. As you head the ball, whip your upper body forward, with your feet coming together to impart power.

If you head the ball at the highest point of your jump, you can better control and direct it, and if the timing is right, you will not lose any power. The force of the ball usually has all the power you need. Direct it well, execute it at the right moment, and your heading will be strong enough to score or to send the ball well upfield.

When preparing to jump for the head ball, quickly step back a few paces, time the ball, and run forward before leaping. This will give you more power and a much higher jump than if you stand in one spot and jump vertically. Smaller players can especially benefit from this kind of running start, and if there is a goalkeeper challenging for the ball, a running approach will give you a better chance of getting up there where his hands are reaching for the ball.

Hang in the air at the peak of your jump the moment you head the ball. Keep your eyes on the ball, and be sure you hit the ball and it doesn't hit you.

Heading Techniques

STRAIGHT-ON LONG BALLS: If the ball is coming straight on and you want to send it back where it came from, meet it with your shoulders square, knees flexed, and upper body bent backward at your waist. Remember, the ball has plenty of force of its own, so timing and aiming it properly are enough to head it effectively.

If you're unchallenged for the ball, decide where you want it to go and whip your body forward, with your power coming from your thighs and your torso. Hit the ball solidly, keeping your eyes on it at all times.

Keeping your eyes on the ball and your feet together, direct the ball back where it came from in a defensive header of a long, high ball.

If the ball is coming from a high boot, such as a goalkeeper's punt or a goal kick, leave the ground slightly at the last moment, dragging one foot as you head the ball. This way you will create a cushion of air between you and the ground, and if you time your head ball correctly, even a towering punt will not hurt when you head it.

Remember to keep your eyes open and direct the ball. You play the ball; it must not play you.

SHOOTING OR CLEARING CROSSES WITH THE HEAD: Time the approaching cross—a ball kicked or thrown from near the sidelines of the field into the goal area—step back a little, and run forward before leaping. Leap off one foot and try to take the ball at the highest point possible in order to get there before your opponents.

Usually these head balls are taken with one shoulder forward, the heading done over that shoulder. Or your upper body is twisted at the moment of impact to whack the ball with ultimate force.

Whether you whip your upper body or flick your head, you must aim the ball. Use the force of the ball's flight, playing it like bumper pool off your forehead toward the goal or out of the penalty box.

Really good players can lean back and give a nod or a flick of the head and get more power. This takes lots of practice and is best learned with a teammate tossing the ball in a low arc while you leap for it and flick it at a target set at a ninety-degree angle from the direction of the toss.

HEADING AGAINST THE GOAL: Whether you're leaping high for a ball or standing alone in front of the net about to nod it home, remember that it's best to head the ball downward. It's too easy to accidentally head the ball over the crossbar, so exaggerate the motion of striking downward with your head. This

Head the ball downward
in a shot on goal.

can be an advantage to the shooter who aims the ball right at the goal line, for the goalkeeper will be defending the ball's downward flight. When the ball hits near the goal line, it bounces upward and is especially difficult for the goalie to judge and to block.

When practicing heading high crosses, start with a partner throwing the ball and work up to longer and longer throws. Then have your partner kick the ball across, intentionally varying the curve and height of the ball.

One of the most dangerous shots on goal comes when an attacker dribbles the ball to the goal line and passes it back in front of the goal. The goalkeeper cannot watch the attacker and the crosser at the same time. Once again, aim this ball and realize that, because it is coming back and is not flying across your path, it can be headed much harder. Aiming it is all you have to do. The force of the turned-back cross is ideal for a powerful header at goal.

DIVING HEADERS: As with most head balls, the power of the ball is all that is needed to give the diving header force. This kind of head ball is seldom planned and is an instinctive reaction, usually as a shot on goal but sometimes as a clearance.

Keep your eyes on the ball and direct it rather than strike it. Again, keep it down. Do not try a diving header into a mass of players. Remember, if you put your head into a dangerous-play situation, the whistle goes against you, and the ball is a free kick for the opponents (see page 000 for rules). Diving headers are effective but are usually done only when there is no other choice. Watch out for flying feet and for goalposts.

When practicing diving headers, have a partner hold the ball. Start from a modified push-up position but with your feet more forward. Lunge up at the ball and head it out of your partner's hands. Snap your head forward to direct the ball. Land on your hands to break the fall.

Have your partner serve different balls—bouncing, straight-ahead, and crosses—all of them playable and fairly easy. Aim your head ball back to the server or at a target.

Gradually develop your power and accuracy. Starting slowly is better than immediately trying difficult moves that result in misses and frustration more often than well-taken head balls.

Keeping It Up

The single best method of learning to head is to keep the ball up with a friend. Start with heading the ball out of your hands, controlling the arc and direction of the header and trying to make it easy for your partner to return the ball. This teaches you to direct the ball from weird and awkward angles. You learn to head on your knees, falling sideways, and backing up, and you begin to understand what it means to give and get a good ball that is playable.

Keep the ball up occasionally with your foot or knee, but keep heading for as long as you can, counting the number of times you and your partner do it. It's simple, it's effective, and it's fun. That's how learning soccer should be.

"Dummy in the Middle"

Often a player takes his eyes off the ball if someone leaps in between. An excellent drill to overcome this tendency is "dummy in the middle," done with two players and a server.

The three players stand in a line, two of them close together and facing the third, who is the server. The server tosses the ball in an arc to the back player, who must jump to head it. The middle player's job is to jump between the ball and the back player, blocking the back player's view of the ball and trying to interfere with a clean jump. The player at the back must watch the ball, leap despite the opponent's presence, and head cleanly back to the server.

Rules can be varied to allow the player in the middle to back into the one who is taking the head ball or to try for the ball, too. Increase the distance between server and receiver, and the force and arc of the toss change to simulate game situations.

This drill teaches you—usually after the served ball bounces off your chest or chin—to watch the ball, not the dummy player in between.

This drill teaches you to keep your eyes on the ball. The server tosses the ball so that it comes down behind the player in the middle . . .

. . . and the receiving player must concentrate on the ball as the middle player leaps close to the ball, without touching it. Try to achieve a clean, well-placed header.

The Shoulder-to-Shoulder Challenge

To learn to keep your balance during a midair collision in the battle for a head ball, stand shoulder-to-shoulder with a partner and leap three times together, counting out loud. On the third jump, collide at the peak of the leap. Do not throw an elbow or use your arm—that's illegal—just collide. When you land, try to keep your balance.

The force of the collision will become stronger with practice. When you jump for a ball in a game, expect that someone else will be doing the same. If you lean into the opponent who also jumps, as this drill teaches, you will hold your position in the air, and when you land, you are more likely to stay on your feet.

This drill can be varied, with players facing each other and colliding the right front of one body against the left front of the other.

Remember, the collision should be in midair at the highest point of the jump. The intent is not to knock the partner over, but to get the feeling of solid body contact, which is so much a part of good soccer, and to avoid being knocked over by it.

 POINTS TO REMEMBER

- Keep your eyes on the ball.
- You attack the ball; don't let the ball hit you.
- Aim the ball where you want it to go.

7 MOVING THE BALL ON OFFENSE

Offense is played both as a team and one-on-one. The individual with the ball decides what to do next, but the larger possibilities are determined by the movements of teammates without the ball.

The ball handler must know what is happening all around the field and be able to give himself enough time to make an effective play; however, no one can successfully complete a pass if teammates do not get open. While good finishing (shooting) moves are usually swift, the buildup to the attack should be controlled. Every move should have a reason, every dribble and every pass a purpose that all members of the attacking team understand. The aim is to get the ball in front of the goal for a shot.

Offensive teammates should move constantly to give the ball handler passing options and to distract defenders and pull them out of position. A mobile offensive team creates confusion because defenders must watch the ball handler and be aware of the rest of the team at the same time.

Moving without the Ball

The most important thing you can do as an offensive player running without (or "off") the ball is to get in position to receive a pass or to create space for someone else who can run in to receive a pass.

If you want to receive a pass, you must run quickly to a spot where the ball handler can get the ball to you. Realize, however, that he must also think it's a good idea to pass—and that's not for you to judge or object to, because you don't have the ball.

Just because you want the ball and no one seems to be defending against you, that doesn't mean you'll get the ball at that moment. You might think you're open, when in fact a defender is well positioned to cut off a pass to you. Or the path of the ball might be blocked because

The player on the right is open and calls for the ball, but the path to him is blocked by the defender.

Now the player has moved left into a position to receive a "square" pass, which is a pass perpendicular to the line of direct attack, here blocked by the defender.

you're not where you should be to receive a clear pass from the ball handler.

Since it's preferable to receive a "square" pass—on the ground and played sharply to you so that the ball is easy to handle and you have time to control it—get to a spot where the ball handler can pass to you without being blocked. You're not considered a good target if, even though there's nobody on you, a defender is close to the ball handler and is blocking the path to you.

When you cut for a pass, expect the ball to be where you're going, not where you are. Get there quickly, preferably at the same time as the ball, and as you run, look around to see what's happening on the field. Before you get the ball, plan what you're going to do with it, or at least have some options in mind.

Collecting a Pass

When a ball is being passed straight to you, you must run toward it, if only for a few steps. This is essential. Moving gives you an advantage over an alert defender who might run toward you hoping to tackle you at the moment you receive.

Also, because you're moving and the ball's moving toward you, your trap will be "alive," making it easier to trick a defender. It's tougher for a defender to know when and where to tackle you if the ball is moving one way and you're moving the other when you take control of it. He has to pause, which gives you an instant to plan your next move.

As soon as you receive the pass and get the ball under control, look up and move it to open space in one motion. If a defender is still chal-

Shield or screen the ball from the defender when you're unable to make an immediate good play.

lenging you, push the ball away and screen it with your body. If a defender comes in fast, throw another fake and cut squarely across the direction of his charge. The defender who is moving fast can't easily change directions, so your move perpendicular to the charge is a simple maneuver that will give you more time to do something offensively with the ball.

Note: Do not move the ball in the same direction the charging defender is going. You'll just have to move away again, and the defender will be more troublesome the longer you waste time trying to get away.

Keep Your Head Up and Look Around

You should know where your teammates and opponents are at all times. You *must* keep your head up and look around. Of course you should keep an eye on the ball at the instant you trap and kick, but try to be looking up while dribbling at full speed or preparing to cross the ball.

If you make a short pass, run to get into position to receive the ball again. As you run, keep your head up and look around. If you call for the ball, look around the field, not just at the ball handler.

As the ball is played to you, quickly scan the field just before you trap it. By knowing where everyone is and where you are with regard to the goal, you have an advantage over the player who only sees the ball and his own feet. You'll also better guess what the defender is thinking, since you're seeing what the defender sees as well as what your teammates are about to do.

To be a top soccer player, you must be aware of what is happening on the field at all times.

Give-and-Go Passing

Short passing and then cutting for a return pass (give-and-go passing) are key to close-quarters soccer. The secret is to make the defender commit to you as you control the ball. Draw the defender closer by faking or by pulling away a little, and when the defender comes in, pass off to your teammate who has moved into an open position.

While taking the ball under control, Lloyd Barker of the American Professional Soccer League's Montreal Impact has his head up, alert for the next play. *Courtesy APSL Didier Constant*

You then cut for a return pass, preferably running behind the player who is defending you, so he can't see you and must spin all the way around to follow you. Cut fast. As you run, don't think of getting the ball back, but think what you'll do with it next when you get it.

If you are the receiver in the give-and-go play, work with the ball handler, who is enticing the defender to come close. Make eye contact with the ball handler. Fake your own defender out by pretending to run one way and then dashing back to get open for the first pass of the give-and-go.

Remember, the return pass in a give-and-go might not be effective if played immediately, first-time. Sometimes it's best to fake the return pass, let your cutting teammate get to a better position, and then slip the pass quickly to him there.

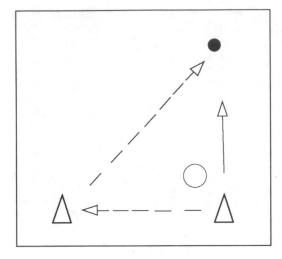

The wall pass: The basic give-and-go is played as if the passer were kicking the ball off a wall and then running around behind the defender to get the ball; the teammate receiving the pass plays the ball first-time into the open space for the passer to receive it.

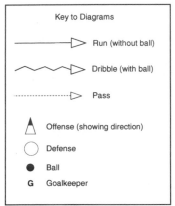

Key to Diagrams

─────▷	Run (without ball)
∿∿∿▷	Dribble (with ball)
·········▷	Pass
△	Offense (showing direction)
○	Defense
●	Ball
G	Goalkeeper

It's usually best to play a ball into an open space, or between defenders, but sometimes the most effective pass is right to a teammate. Then you sprint, cutting for a return pass.

When there are lots of players close together, direct passing to teammates' feet keeps the ball under your team's control until the moment someone cuts into the open and gets a pass through.

The Long Pass versus the Short Pass

There is nothing more beautiful in soccer than a long pass perfectly played to a charging forward who follows with a quick shot on goal.

Some people, however, scorn every long pass as unskillful, wasteful, or downright bad soccer. Maybe it's because they never learned how to do it properly themselves. If so, they've missed a wonderful aspect of soccer, different from everything else in the game, and magnificent when done well. A mixture of long and short passes is essential for any soccer team to be effective.

Youth soccer, where players have less ball-control skill, can be played effectively with long balls that are chased down by the forwards. Then the short passing and dribbling follows—but down near the other team's goal, where the scoring is to be done.

No amount of short passing or back passing has the dramatic offensive power of the deep ball, on the ground or in the air, that splits the defense and sends an attacker in for a thrilling shot.

Playing the Long Ball

It is essential that a medium or long pass that gets through or over the defense be playable by an attacking teammate running after it. Therefore, the ball should have backspin.

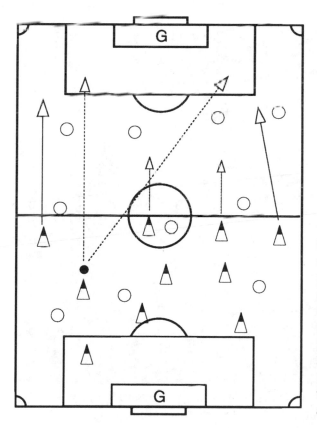

Long passes: If aimed well, or if the forwards are strong in the air, the long high pass is devastating against any defense. Repeated long passes pressure the defense again and again, causing mistakes and wearing down the defenders, who are constantly backpedaling or racing to beat swift attackers to the ball. Two vulnerable areas are the front corners of the penalty box, where an attacker can take a shot on the run or can first-time a cross for a teammate to run onto.

Hitting a ball with backspin causes it to float, to rise a little higher than expected, and often to drift maddeningly over the defender's leap to head it down. The backspin also makes the ball seem to stop when it lands, preventing it from rolling away to be picked up by the goalie. With backspin, as the ball hits the ground it slows a little, hanging, so that the attacker has an easier time bringing it under control.

To make a ball lift and then spin backward to die at your teammate's feet, do the following:

Stand a few long steps back from the ball, then approach for the kick. Lean back and away on your nonkicking foot's side, and keep your nonkicking foot well behind the ball. Kick the lower half of the ball, chipping under it without following through. This means you end your kick by striking the ground slightly with the inside of your foot, thus giving the ball backspin.

As with the lofted pass, the long ball should have spin (usually backspin) to make it easier for the receiver to control. Lean away and hit the lower half of the ball.

Practice this against a kickboard, without taking the approach steps. Just stand there and chip, over and over again. Be careful not to kick the ground too hard, but be sure to get under the ball.

Do it right and the technique will lift a dead or nonmoving ball high. Do this with power, or to a moving ball on a soccer field, and you'll send a floater, one of the most dangerous offensive kicks of all.

This technique is also good for lofting long free kicks, particularly corner kicks. Impart a curve to the ball by hitting it more to the outside; it will turn in toward your teammate and away from the goalie, making it more difficult to save.

POINTS TO REMEMBER

- Do not wait for a pass; move toward the ball as it is coming to you.
- Keep your head up and look around as much as possible, whether you have the ball or not.
- Get open for a pass, but don't expect a pass if the ball handler is blocked by a defender.
- Lean back and hit low on the ball to help put backspin on a long pass, lofting the ball and making it die at your teammate's feet.

8 DEFENSE AND TACKLING

As with offense, defense is played both as a team and one-on-one.

When you are defending against an attacker who has the ball, you must be sure the rest of the defensive team is covering other attackers to prevent the ball handler from making a pass. If you know your teammates are working to cover other attackers, then you also know that the ball handler will have trouble finding someone to pass to. That makes your own defensive efforts all the more effective and puts the player with the ball under pressure.

Of course, if your teammates do not mark their opponents, and you are the only one covering an attacker, then your task is more difficult. A lazy defensive team allows the ball handler to have passing options. One defender on the ball handler can't stop every pass. If the ball handler fakes a pass and you try to block it, you will be thrown off balance. The attacker can more easily dribble around you.

The Defender Must Win the Initiative

Theoretically, the person with the ball has the advantage; however, you as a defender must take the initiative and make the ball handler react to you and do what you want. As a defender, you must think and act as if you were in control of the game.

Let's say your team is on defense and tightly marking the attackers. You are in the midfield, facing an attacker coming toward you with the ball. The attacker must watch you, look for a place to pass, and keep the ball under control. You now are defending one-on-one.

The first thing you should do is approach the dribbler as fast as you can, not allowing him any time to look up and see the field. As you come in, fake a tackle. Pretend to go for the ball, keeping your balance, but do not commit yourself unless you're sure you have a clean shot at the ball.

Once you've forced the attacker to turn his back to you, move in close and do not allow the attacker to turn again. Lean in, but do not charge illegally.

This accomplishes two things:

1. The attacker is forced to react to your fake and often will move in the direction you want him to.
2. You begin to gain the initiative, taking control of the situation away from the dribbler.

Make the fake convincing enough to force the attacker to turn his back to you. Now get up very close, lightly touching the attacker, and poke your foot in to try to get the ball.

Pressure the Ball Handler

The best defense, of course, is to prevent your opponent from getting the ball. Mark closely when on defense, keeping goalside of the attacker who wants a pass. You want to cut off a direct pass to the player you're covering, and you want to stay a couple of steps closer to the goal than your opponent in case there's a through pass or a long-ball lead pass.

But if your opponent does succeed in getting the ball, stay close to him. Keep your balance. Do not commit to one side or the other. Pressure the ball handler, and don't let him turn around. No one can score while facing the wrong direction. Protect the inside so the dribbler cannot turn and pass through toward the goal.

Do not allow yourself to be outmaneuvered. Keep your chest close to the ball handler's back, and keep poking your foot in, trying to knock the ball away. Always be able to see the ball.

If the ball handler's teammates are covered, he is in a bind. The fans will yell for the ball handler to do something. His teammates will get rattled, trying to get open. The momentum is now on the side of the defensive team. A teammate of yours should challenge from the other side, forcing the ball handler to withdraw, harassed from two sides.

Always try to get two defenders on the ball after the dribbler's back is turned. Generally you will be able to get the ball, knock it loose, or force the ball handler to pass it away and thus momentarily break up the attack. If you do this again and again, the other team will never be able to develop a strong attack.

- If your opponent gets the ball, immediately force him to turn his back to you, facing away from the goal you are defending.
- Be patient; remember, the attacker has to beat you, but you don't have to do anything. Keep balanced and don't commit until you decide to win the ball.
- Move in close to prevent the ball handler from turning toward the goal; keep up the pressure by physical contact, making sure not to shove with your chest, which is illegal. Kick with little stabs at the ball to knock it loose.
- If your opponent tries to dribble around you, do not wildly tackle unless you're in a desperation situation—if the ball handler has you beaten and is passing you.

Play Both the Ball and the Ball Handler

When defending against a dribbler, instead of overcommitting with a lunge for the ball, block his path. Do not just play the ball; play the ball and your opponent at the same time.

Get as close as possible to the ball handler. Never tackle from too far away or you will be overstretched and off balance.

Throw a fake to force the dribbler to go one way or the other. As the dribbler moves, block his path by reaching with your leg *and your shoulder* so that your leg blocks the ball and your shoulder blocks his chest. Do not tackle with just your foot or your leg. Even if you get a foot on the ball, the momentum of the ball handler will likely pull the ball through and he will remain in control, leaving you off balance and beaten.

Take the dribbler's charge on the point of your shoulder, but do not thrust your shoulder into the dribbler's chest, which is illegal. Position yourself so that the dribbler's momentum carries him into your solidly planted defensive position. Keep your center of gravity low, and hold this position. The dribbler must get around you to avoid the collision. This situation tends to favor you, the defender, and while the off-balance dribbler is trying to get clear, the ball is bouncing loose, and you are on balance, able to pick it up or boot it away.

In tackling, let the ball handler come close enough so when you seem to take his fake . . .

. . . you are in fact able to reach the ball when he cuts . . .

First Break Up the Attack, Then Get the Ball

Your first object on defense is to break up an attack. Your second is to come up with the ball.

If, after you tackle, the dribbler still has the ball, try to force him to turn his back to the goal you are defending. If he tries to beat you again, repeat the process: Fake a tackle and force the dribbler to the side you choose. When you are close enough, keep your balance and reach with your leg and shoulder to block his path. Take the full momentum of the dribbler's move on your shoulder and block the dribble.

If you are beaten by the ball, at least that's better than being beaten by the ball *and* the dribbler. With the proper tackle, the dribbler is blocked, and often the ball is, too. If you block the path of the dribbler and the ball squirts through, your defensive teammate can scoop it up.

. . . and you play dribbler and ball at the same time. Actually, the dribbler's movement carries him into you, so you're not fouling. It is essential to block with your shoulder and leg together—again, being sure to play the ball so as not to foul.

Your shoulder winds up taking the full force of the attacker's chest because the attacker is trying to dribble while keeping the ball and his balance.

POINTS TO REMEMBER

- Block the ball and the opposing player at the same time.
- Force the dribbler wide and off the ball.
- Let the dribbler's momentum carry him against your shoulder, and do not yield an inch when the contact occurs.
- Keep your center of gravity—and your shoulder—as low as possible and use the strength of your legs to push yourself upward to meet your opponent's move.

SOLE-OF-THE-FOOT TACKLE: Sometimes when the ball handler is coming straight on at the goal, and you as the defender are too late to force him to move away or turn, all you can do is block the shot with the sole of your foot.

This must be done decisively, for if the shot does get off, you might find the ball in your gut. The sole of your foot takes the force of the shot before the full power of the shot is let loose.

In soccer, going in hard and taking the force of the ball just as it is kicked is less painful than taking it when the ball has gained velocity. Hesitation will result in the ball striking you full force. Decisiveness and hard tackling deflect the ball before it can get going.

THE SLIDING TACKLE: The sliding tackle is a desperation lunge, used by the defender only when he has been beaten. It is illegal if done from behind the attacker.

Blocking the ball with a sole-of-the-foot tackle.

From about ten feet away, lunge with your outside leg at the ball, aiming ahead of it. The ball is either pushed away or blocked by your sliding leg. Be sure to play only the ball and not the attacker.

If you miss with a sliding tackle, however, you are out of the play, and the attacker has broken through.

THE SHOULDER CHARGE: In some defensive situations you may find yourself running alongside your opponent while he is pushing the ball ahead. This is a good time for the shoulder charge. Better yet, let your opponent do the charging and you hold firm to your position. Lean into and a little ahead of your opponent so that he must counter with a shoulder against yours. This will break your opponent's control of the ball, and you will find yourself momentarily between him and the ball.

A clean shoulder charge is essential in good soccer. It is a matter of leaning, positioning yourself for the force of your opponent's move, and holding your ground in the collision that follows. Make sure you are lower than your opponent whenever possible, because your lower center of gravity gives you stability and strength.

You can collide shoulders as long as your opponent has one foot on the ground, but if your opponent is leaping, then leaning in with your shoulder is illegal and can be a dangerous move, called a submarine.

Effective Tackle Practice

There is no better way to develop tackling skills than to play small-sided games with a wall, kick-return screen, or a kickboard. One-on-one games are also valuable in developing defensive ability. The ball handler has to dribble, and you as the defender have to come in tightly to prevent a quick shot.

Try this effective one-on-one game: The attacker starts dribbling from behind a certain line. If you steal the ball, you can shoot it. If the attacker shoots and misses and you get the rebound, you must take the ball back behind the starting line before being allowed to attack.

POINTS TO REMEMBER

- Make the dribbler go the way you want; be sure to throw fakes as you approach him.
- Your first objective on defense is to make the dribbler turn his back to the goal you're defending.
- Do not tackle until you're close enough to win the ball; keep your balance.
- Move in with your leg and shoulder, and block both the ball and the dribbler at the same time.
- When tackling, do not reach for the ball where it is but where you think it's going to be after the dribbler makes a move.
- Keep your center of gravity lower than your opponent's.

9 OFFSIDES, FREE KICKS, AND THROW-INS

For all of soccer's constant action and movement, there are many times in a game when play stops and the ball is put down for an unchallenged free kick. These situations, when taken advantage of, can mean the difference between winning and losing.

Along with throw-ins, free kicks are commonly called "restarts" and are plays that should do one of two things: lead to a shot on goal, or at the very least maintain ball possession by the kicking team.

Offsides

This simple but controversial rule says that a player in the opponent's half of the field is offsides if, when the ball is played by his team, the player is nearer the opponent's goal than the ball. Offsides keeps attackers from hanging around the goalmouth, snuffs out promising attacks, and even causes apparent goals to be disallowed (see chapter 14 for diagrams).

The player is not offsides if

1. There are at least two defenders between the player and the goal.
2. The ball was last touched by a defender.
3. The player touched the ball last.
4. The player received the ball directly from a corner kick, goal kick, throw-in, or drop ball.

If an attacking player is called offsides by the referee, play stops and the defending team gets a free kick at the point where the infraction occurred. Offsides is a judgment call, and the rule can be interpreted differently.

The rule makes the attacker wait before being allowed to sprint past the defenders to receive a through pass. Once the ball has been kicked, the attacker is no longer offsides and may go, even if he is running ahead of the ball. (If the ball is ahead of the attacker, the attacker cannot be offsides, since the ball is closer to the goal than he is.)

In plays in front of the goal, officials usually will not call a player offsides who is out of the play, for example on the wing, and not distracting the goalkeeper. But the offsides rule is open to interpretation and causes frustration to players and fans alike.

However, offsides is a fact of life that favors the defense, and a good defense makes the most of it. Defenders will coordinate their movement upfield at a given signal and place an unsuspecting attacker offsides. Of course, if the officials do not catch this forced offsides and the attacker gets away with it, a goal can be scored.

Free Kicks

Free kicks are awarded to a team when the opponent fouls or is offsides. Most free kicks happen at midfield, well away from the goal, and the kicker's team must attempt to keep possession of the ball.

The defensive team must be at least ten yards away from the ball when a free kick is taken. Before the ball can be touched again by anyone, it must first be allowed to roll its complete circumference.

When calling for the free kick, the referee will declare whether the kick is "direct" or "indirect." A direct kick can be shot right into the goal for a score. An indirect kick must touch at least one other player

Montreal Impact forward Pierre-Richard Thomas takes a free kick, head down, planted foot back from the ball, and leaning away so that the ball will be lofted into the opponent's goal area. *Courtesy APSL Didier Constant*

on either team before going into the goal. In most cases an indirect kick is turned into a scoring attempt by one player pushing the ball a few feet to a teammate who then shoots at goal.

The direct kick, when close enough to the goal, is a golden opportunity for a good shooter to wind up and hammer the ball. Even if the goalie makes a desperate save, the offensive team will at least get a chance at the rebound.

With a direct kick it is important that the offensive team know where the kicker is going with the ball. Practice direct kicks with offensive players on the field. Anticipate rebounds. Also, attackers must remember not to move offsides before the ball is kicked.

When the free kick is indirect, the kicker and teammates should also know from practice where the ball is going. Sometimes two players charge the ball as if to shoot, then step over it while a third comes in quickly and kicks it. But whatever play is used, it is important that everyone know the plan.

A BASIC INDIRECT PLAY: The most fundamental and effective indirect kick is to chip the ball toward the far goalpost, out of the goalie's reach. Then an attacker runs in and heads the ball downward across the goalmouth. By playing the ball downward, past the goalie, the header gives another attacker the chance to push the ball into the net.

Putting the ball into play in front of the goalmouth like this is better than trying to head the ball directly into the goal. For one thing, as the player heading the ball moves toward the goal, the goalkeeper will instinctively try to block a direct shot on goal. Furthermore, heading a ball into the goal from such a sharp angle is difficult to do.

The defense probably knows what is supposed to happen, but if attackers get a head on the ball and send it in front of the goalmouth, it is extremely difficult to clear the ball. Try this five or six times a game and you'll surely get a goal.

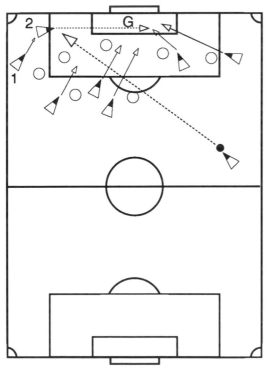

A free-kick play: A simple and effective free-kick play is to loft the ball into the far side of the penalty box, where a teammate then heads it down across the goalmouth; the goalie and defenders are expecting the header to be aimed at the goal, but the attackers know the ball will be played in front of the goal, giving them the advantage of knowing where the ball will go.

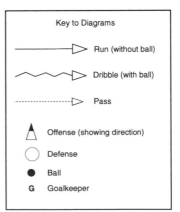

Key to Diagrams

———————▷ Run (without ball)

∿∿∿∿∿▷ Dribble (with ball)

·············▷ Pass

△ Offense (showing direction)

◯ Defense

● Ball

G Goalkeeper

DIRECT SHOTS: When shooting a direct kick from the range of eighteen to thirty yards, keeping the ball in play is of major importance. That means putting it on goal. Even if the ball is saved, it often will be knocked down and bounce around in front of the goalmouth.

It is always difficult to score directly from a long free kick, but your best shot is one directed at the far corner of the goal. The goalie will usually line up hard against the near post to protect against a straight shot, but a curving fast-paced shot at the far side of the goal is almost impossible to stop if it is accurately placed. If blocked, the ball will still fall near the goalmouth for a rebound shot.

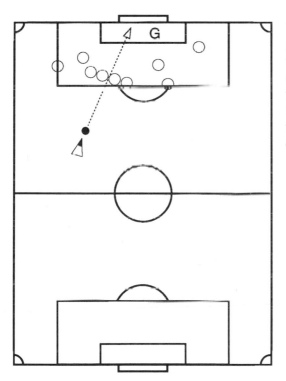

The defensive wall: At the direction of the goalkeeper, players in the wall position themselves to block the kicker's clear view of one side of the goal, and the goalkeeper takes a position to cover the other side. Other defenders are positioned to cut off through passes or to get balls that bounce off or over the wall.

POINTS TO REMEMBER

- Direct kicks can be shot right into the goal.
- Indirect kicks require another player from either team to touch the ball before it goes into the goal.

- On either direct or indirect kicks, the offensive team should know what the kicker is going to do with the ball.
- Free kicks at goal, aimed accurately at the goalmouth, should force the goalie or a defender to knock the ball down for another attacker to shoot.

Corner Kicks

When a ball crosses the goal line outside the goalposts and is last touched by the defensive team, a corner kick is awarded. As with other restart kicks, the corner kick should be practiced by the entire team so that everyone knows what is supposed to happen.

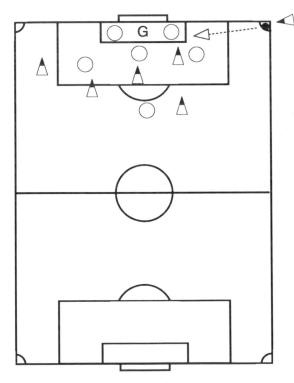

The corner kick: Attackers should position themselves out far enough so they have room to charge in on the corner kick; attackers should not start so close to the goal that the ball goes over their heads.

HIGH CORNER KICKS: The corner kick is most effective when the ball goes too high for the goalie to reach, has backspin, and drops into the penalty area for an attacker to shoot. This shot requires lots of practice and a strong but delicate touch to put the right spin, height, and speed on the ball.

Use backspin when lofting a ball to make it drop and stay where it hits the ground. A good header should be positioned just outside the penalty box to run in and jump for the high corner kick. Even if the head ball does not go in, it will be put into play around the goalmouth, as long as the header keeps the ball down when trying to score.

CURVING CORNER KICKS: Sometimes a strong shooter taking a corner kick will rip the ball with outside spin and curve it right at the goalmouth, close to one of the goalposts. A corner kick is a direct kick, so scoring this way is possible. However, this type of corner usually results in rebounds, which provide the attacking team with another chance to score.

SHORT CORNER KICKS: Corners are sometimes taken short, aimed for a teammate who at the last moment runs toward the kicker and gets a pass. This player then dribbles fast across the penalty box, drawing defenders out of the goal area and opening space for a pass or shot from a better angle. The risk here is that offensive players will be caught offsides. The advantage is that a skillful attacker can make a pass from closer in or take a shot at the far goalpost from the near corner of the penalty box.

Goal Kicks

Taken by a defender after the offensive team has knocked the ball out-of-bounds over the end line, or goal line, the goal kick is one of the most important free kicks of all.

If the kick is weak and the other team intercepts it, the ball will come right back again, usually to a defense that is not ready and finds itself overwhelmed and trapped in its own half of the field.

LONG GOAL KICKS: When the goal kick is a long one accurately played to a teammate who can handle it or can head it, there is no better way to start an attack. Most of the opposing team is bypassed by the long goal kick, and the few remaining defenders will find themselves challenged at the midfield line.

To make a successful long goal kick, make sure your foot connects with the ball just below center. Keep your head down and your eyes on the ball, as always, and aim the ball at a target.

Goal kicks for distance should be executed with some backspin, but you need power, too. Therefore, instead of not following through as with the lofted backspin kick, you should fly forward, off the ground, in the follow-through.

Consistent practice at long kicks will develop the rhythm and follow-through that give the kicker power. When working with a kick return, concentrate on the follow-through and on hitting the ball just below center.

SHORT GOAL KICKS: Teams with skillful defensive ball handlers like to make short plays from the goal kick, keeping the ball and pushing it with a series of passes upfield to a teammate playing offense. The short goal kick may not be touched by anyone until it leaves the penalty box, so it must be taken quickly and accurately.

The risk of short goal kicks is that an opponent might intercept the ball deep in your territory. The advantage is that your team maintains ball control until the moment a decisive through pass is played for a final attack on goal.

Kickoffs

The purpose of the kickoff is, first and foremost, to obtain possession of the ball. The forwards should not expect to make a break for goal immediately after receiving the kickoff, because there are too many opponents to beat.

On the kickoff, the ball must travel forward its circumference before it can be touched again. Good defenders will charge in on the kickoff and try to surround the player who gets the ball first. Therefore, it's best to play the ball immediately back to a midfielder who is far enough away to have time to handle it before the defense swarms in.

The kickoff should be sharply played, and the pass to the midfielder should be strong, yet easy to handle, and go where the midfielder wants it. The midfielder should know which teammates are going where—a wing forward breaking behind the opposite midfielders and in front of the fullbacks, or a midfield teammate staying close for a possible pass.

A good team consistently controls the ball after the kickoff. The ball starts at midfield, and if strikers are given time to penetrate the defense before finishing passes are made from the midfielders, a kickoff can result in shots on goal.

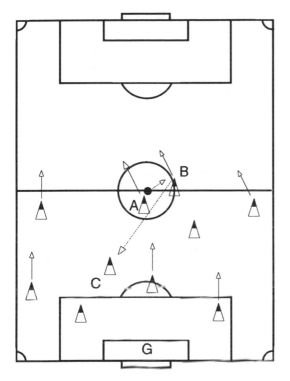

A kickoff play: A plays the ball to B, who sharply sends it on the ground to C, who holds the ball just long enough for teammates to move into position for a medium pass. The object of a kickoff is to keep control of the ball, then to begin an attack on goal, in this case down the left side of the field, where the attackers move to receive the pass from C.

 ## POINTS TO REMEMBER

- The kickoff is only the first movement in the buildup for an attack, and forwards should seldom try to dribble up the middle.
- The team should know where the ball is going and how the attack is to be built.
- Midfielders should maintain control of the ball by short passing and so give strikers a chance to get close to the goal.

Throw-ins

Although throwing the ball directly into the goal for a score is not permitted, the throw-in can be an excellent offensive weapon in the attacking third of the field. Strong throwers can put the ball into the goal-mouth for teammates to head in. Most often, the throw-in is played directly to a teammate who then passes or makes a run for the goal.

Like the kickoff, the most important part of throwing in is keeping the ball in your team's possession. Usually a team has a set play for throw-ins, but the rule of thumb is to make the ball easy to handle. Throw so the ball lands at your teammate's feet, not at his midsection or shins, and so that the receiver can easily shield the ball from a marking defender.

FEET TOGETHER: The throw-in must be taken with your feet parallel, pointing at the sideline, the ball held in both hands. Your hands must be at the sides of the ball, thumbs not touching. With both feet on the ground, bring the ball back directly over your head, sling it forward, again directly over your head, and release it behind or above your head. The ball is thrown with a whipping movement of your arms, not by flicking your wrists or hands.

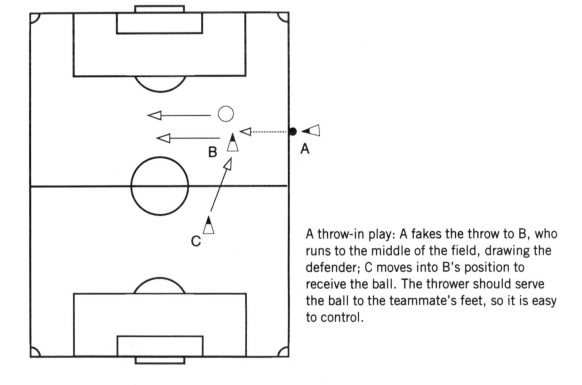

A throw-in play: A fakes the throw to B, who runs to the middle of the field, drawing the defender; C moves into B's position to receive the ball. The thrower should serve the ball to the teammate's feet, so it is easy to control.

Your arms must follow through completely, while your upper body remains upright to avoid a foul throw. The ball should not spin—intentionally or inadvertently—or the officials will call a foul throw, declaring the ball was thrown with one hand and not two.

SCISSOR MOVEMENT OF THE FEET: The throw can also be taken with one foot behind the other. Your back foot is scissored forward and dragged along the ground at the moment of the throw to increase power.

Sometimes the thrower takes a little run for more power, and often the throw is faked to another player before being delivered to the target player.

 POINTS TO REMEMBER

- Lean well back at your knees and whip your upper body forward with the throw.
- Stay upright and do not lean forward after you throw.
- Aim for your teammate's feet on a bounce or two, not at his chest or head unless such a throw is expected.

Throw-ins are taken with both feet on the ground and pointing toward the field, the ball brought above and behind your head. Arch your body back for power . . .

. . . and release the ball from behind your head.

The complete follow-through is necessary
both for power and to make the throw legal.

10 POSITIONS AND TEAMWORK

Which position do you want to play?

Everyone obviously likes to score, to be the hero. So you want to be the striker, dribbling past three or four defenders to beat the goalie with a spectacular shot.

That sounds good, but there are ten other positions on a team, all of them just as important as striker. Each position requires particular skills and abilities and offers its own special satisfaction. How do your abilities compare with the requirements of the position?

If you are fast and strong, are able to head and shoot from all positions, and have a "nose for goals," a natural ability to be in the right place to score, then perhaps you should be a striker.

Or maybe you are a good ball handler who can run all day, who takes satisfaction in taking a ball away, who likes to outguess the attacker and intercept a pass, and who really enjoys giving the striker a perfect pass that sets up a goal. If that's the case, you should be a midfielder.

At midfield you won't often get the glory of scoring, but you will get to handle the ball more often than anyone else. You'll play offense and defense, and now and again you'll score with a long shot or a quick surprise shot.

Or maybe you love to head the ball, to take long, accurate kicks, to feel like a defensive rock. Maybe you are a player who is hard to beat on the ground or in the air. Sounds like a good attitude for a stopper or fullback. You'll be defending your own goal and making spectacular saves on the goal line, just when everyone thought the goalies were beaten.

The real star of the soccer team, though, is the goalkeeper, who, like the pitcher in baseball, is the team leader. No matter how good the field players are, the goalkeeper's ability and personality can determine the team's success.

There's more to soccer than scoring goals. Each position is unique, with its own demands and its own satisfactions.

Whether on offense or defense, soccer players have to understand how to use their bodies to keep opponents from the ball. Here, the Montreal Impact's Abdel Sahrane, left, battles with Brian Haynes of the Colorado Foxes, both fighting for control of the space around the ball. *Courtesy APSL Didier Constant*

The Striker

It used to be that the main attackers were three players who stayed up front, the center forward in the middle and one on each wing. Their first task when they had the ball was not scoring, however, but getting the ball upfield. They had to outsmart the defenders and skillfully distribute the ball to others for clear shots. This meant these players were often far upfield, waiting, when the other team was attacking, so they were out of the defensive effort.

In time, soccer systems have changed so that more players have been brought back on defense and into the midfield. The new systems are more defensive, so only two players—or sometimes only one—lead the attack.

Called a "striker" because of the expectation that he will concentrate on breakaways and shots at the goal, this player is usually a powerful athlete. The striker stays in the front but roves from side to side, trying to get away from tight-marking defenders and moving to get open for a pass.

The striker has to be ready to outrun the defense and chase deep passes up the middle, as well as dribble with skill and determination through a packed defense and shoot hard and accurately. Mentally, the striker must have a strong will, self-confidence, and a sure instinct for what he does on the field.

The center forward of years ago often was expected to be an excellent distributor of the ball, someone who could dribble until the time was right to pass off for another player to shoot. Although this skill is still important, the striker of today is more than ever expected to be a one-on-one player who can get to the ball, keep it, and shoot it.

The Midfielder

The ideal midfielder is unselfish and versatile. He is often the team's best ball handler, good at head balls, tackling, and setting up attackers with passes that lead to shots on goal.

The midfielder must be able to follow the attack and pick up the other team's clearances, should know when to take a shot or even when to dribble up the middle and shoot. He must be able to recover against a counterattack and sprint back on defense.

The midfielder does not tire easily, physically or mentally. This player is expected to break up the opposing team's attack in the penalty box and make an outlet pass, then to follow for the return pass and take off up the field, eighty yards, on the attack. In the next moment, he is back on defense, running to cover a teammate who is tackling a ball handler, or trying to slow down the counterattack.

More than anyone else, the midfielder must be in top condition and must know what to do with the ball and be able to anticipate the opposition's next move. Soccer games are usually won or lost at midfield. The team that controls midfield, whose midfield players are consistently setting one another up or shutting the other team down, will often win the game.

Fullbacks and Stoppers

Although the best defenders on professional or college soccer teams are always excellent ball handlers, youth team defenders are usually less skilled but physically strong and tough. Defenders must be brave and decisive, as well as good at straight-ahead kicking, first-time kicking, and head balls. On good youth teams, defenders are encouraged to dribble now and again, and sometimes to attack and take a shot.

Good players understand how to cover each other on defense, and midfield players from the other side of the field will drop back when a deep defender leaves the defensive position and makes an offensive play.

Whether youth or professional, defense requires the athlete to be a true team player, cool under pressure and fearless. The best defender wants the attacker to try to dribble past so he can take the ball away. There is nothing better than a defensive player who can steal the ball and make an offensive run. When a fullback comes up with the ball and dribbles out of the back into the opponent's midfield, the other team is hard-pressed to get back on defense quickly enough to stop him.

It's difficult to beat a team that has defenders who consistently come up with the ball at midfield and then make controlled passes toward the goal. First, of course, the defender has to be good enough to

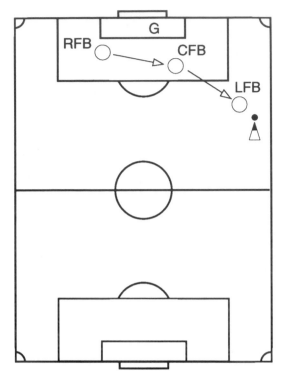

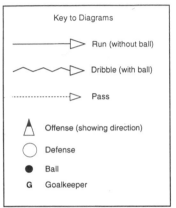

The defensive shift: Without this instinctive teamwork, the defense has no flexibility or depth. In this diagram, the center fullback (CFB) comes across to support the left fullback (LFB), and the right fullback (RFB) takes the central defensive position, so the area in front of the goal is protected.

Key to Diagrams

⟶▷ Run (without ball)

〜〜▷ Dribble (with ball)

------▷ Pass

△ Offense (showing direction)

○ Defense

● Ball

G Goalkeeper

get the ball, either with a skillful tackle or by anticipating and cutting off a pass.

As with any good soccer player, the good defender is always looking around to see where teammates and opponents are, trying to anticipate what they will do next, and just as important, asking, "What will I do with the ball if I get it?"

The defender's first task is to prevent the opponent from getting the ball. When forced back toward the goal area, however, the defender must think first of protecting a zone. The final defensive zone is, if necessary, behind the goalkeeper.

Real soccer fans and players love watching good defense just as much as they like seeing goals scored.

The Sweeper Back

Some teams play with a sweeper back, who is positioned behind the last line of defense and is responsible for intercepting penetrating passes and for blocking the path of an attacker who has broken through. This player moves from side to side to support the fullbacks and to anticipate the opponent's breakaway moves.

The sweeper must be able to kick long clearances with confidence and be hard to beat with dribbling. Often faced with defending against long high crosses, he should be a solid header and courageous in one-on-one collisions.

Sometimes the sweeper can move forward with or without the ball, but usually only to get open to make a pass. He then immediately retires behind the defensive backs and watches for the next attack coming downfield.

The sweeper should be an intelligent and skillful playmaker whose passes start attacks.

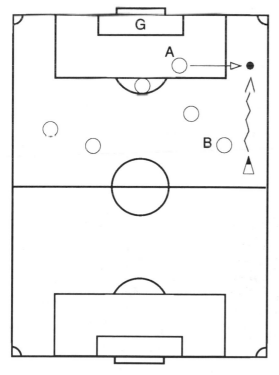

The sweeper back: The sweeper back, A, must anticipate attackers breaking through the defense. The sweeper quickly challenges the attacker, not necessarily tackling, but always blocking the path to the goal and giving other defenders time to recover and move into position.

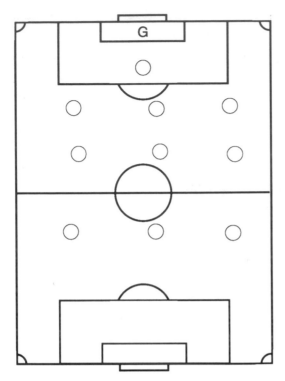

The sweeper system: The sweeper back gives depth to the defense, cutting off through balls and delaying dribblers who break through defenders. Having three midfielders makes it easier to dominate that aspect of the game, but takes one striker away from the attack.

The Rover

Often a team is set up so that one very good player has the task of playing all over the midfield, from penalty area to penalty area. This player is known as a rover, a free player who is the brain—and sometimes the heart—of a team. The rover must be an outstanding soccer player in top condition, someone who takes as much pleasure in tackling as in setting up a goal. The rover should also be able to take a shot at the right time.

Even more than the average midfielder, the rover has to run hard. Generally, the rover does not mark the same player all game long, but helps defenders or appears as the first point of the defense to harass the opposing ball handler.

On defense the rover must be the one who first meets the opponent's attack. On offense, the rover must get open for a pass and must be around the ball all the time.

Defensive players who have the ball will look for the rover when they want to send the first pass in the transition from defense to offense. Forwards with the ball often look back for the rover to come sprinting upfield, appearing as if from nowhere to take a pass back from them.

The rover has the freedom to look around and survey the situation. That freedom of movement also allows the rover to follow teammates on the attack and spot an opportunity for a through pass that sets up a shot on goal.

The rover is often a team leader. Only the goalkeeper is more essential to a team's success on the field.

The Goalkeeper

There's a saying that a weak goalie makes a good team bad, and a good goalie makes a weak team good. The goalie must be a superb athlete, always brave and at times a little reckless. A goalie who is indecisive will too often be caught out of position or be late getting to the ball.

It's better to have a goalie who is too aggressive and goes out to get the ball a little too much than a goalie who stays in the goalmouth, letting the other team take easy shots unchallenged. The keeper who makes key saves will lift his team's confidence and will frustrate the opponents and shake their confidence. An ordinary performance by players in the field can be overpowering when the goalie is saving the other team's best shots time and again.

The goalie must be emotionally stable—getting scored on must not crush his ego, and teammates must never be blamed for goals being scored.

Building a team begins with defense, and defense begins with the goalkeeper. No position in soccer is more difficult, and no player is more respected by those who understand the game.

Teamwork

There are many systems in soccer—some keyed for defense, others for offense. But no system can work if the players are unable to adhere to its requirements.

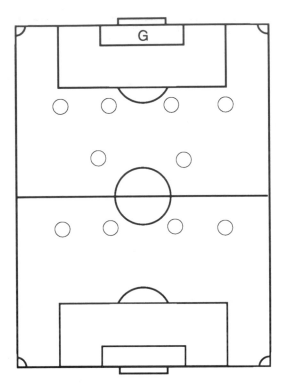

The 4–2–4 System: Strong on defense and offense, with four players in each position, this system requires two outstanding and tireless midfielders to control the attacking game and get back to support the defense.

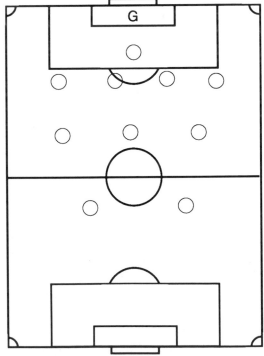

The catenaccio system: Catenaccio (meaning "chain"), with four backs and a sweeper, was developed by the Italians in the late sixties. It creates a powerful defense and requires fast strikers who can break away and get that one goal needed to win. Variations call for one of the four fullbacks to go up on attack or into the midfield from time to time.

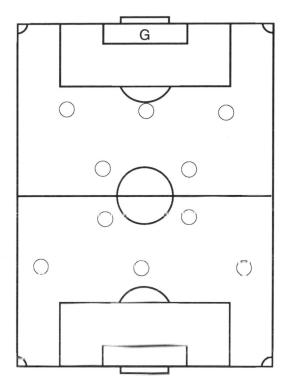

The W-M system: This was the most basic formation used from the twenties to the sixties, the two inside forwards forming a square at midfield with the two wing halfbacks; the center halfback is withdrawn between the two fullbacks. Thus, the defensive five form a "W" while the offensive five form an "M." If a team wants a stronger defensive formation, a midfielder is drawn back to fullback, and a forward drawn back to midfield.

Therefore, a good coach organizes his or her team and develops a system of play according to the players' abilities. The basics of creating a team can be described simply as building from the center out: First find the goalkeeper, then the middle deep defender, then the key striker at center forward.

Next come the midfielders—the workhorses of the team—then the fullbacks to work with the midfielders. After that come decisions about using extra attacking forwards or extra midfielders or a sweeper fullback. If the players are in the best positions—based on their temperament, ability, and inclination—then the team will begin to shape itself.

After the coach finds the right players for all the positions, the team learns to play together according to a broad plan.

Try to play as many positions as possible if you want to become a better all-around player. It will also help you appreciate and understand the tasks your teammates have to do.

No one who has once been a goalkeeper will become angry when the goalie lets in a goal. No one who has missed an easy scoring chance will criticize the center forward for putting one over the bar.

There are times when a team needs you at one position when you'd like to play another. Talk it out with your coach and let him know how you feel. Perhaps you can split time at different positions, or you can decide that for this season you'll learn to be the best you can at the position the coach wants you to play.

11 GOALKEEPING

In addition to his duties between the goalposts, a goalkeeper should know how to play soccer in the field. While you might have the natural physical and mental assets that could make you a good goalie, concentrate first on becoming a good all-around soccer player. No matter how much you're complimented for your abilities in the net, do not let yourself be so flattered that you never learn how to play the complete game.

The best goalies understand what's happening on the field and are able to tell when an attacker is about to break through, make a pass, or take a shot. That understanding, which comes only from playing in the field, makes the goalie effective in coming out to cut off crosses or take the ball off a forward's dribbling feet.

Goalies who cannot play in the field are unable to recognize what the defenders and attackers are doing. No matter how athletic the goalie is, or how brave and quick, he will be unable to stop a shot or pass that is unexpected because he did not have the intuition to "read" the play.

The Goalie's Domain

When you're learning to be a goalkeeper, you must think like one, and that means being decisive, confident, and calm. Realize you own the penalty box. It's your domain, and any ball that comes in there is yours. Any attacker who comes in there with it is going to lose it. You want the offense to shoot. You love making saves, especially making difficult saves look easy.

You must be in charge mentally and physically when your team is defending. Call to teammates, tell them where to go and when you are coming for the ball. They should let you have the ball when you call for it, and they should get out of your way when you make your move.

Physically you should be strong and quick, agile and acrobatic. Mentally you should be self-assured, not afraid to risk failure, and always willing to rise to the challenge with every ounce of courage and determination.

No goalie is allowed to blame his teammates when scored upon. Every goalie must be the rock of a team's defense and the source of a team's confidence. It's a tall order for anyone to fill, but once you've filled it, you'll never forget the joy of playing goalkeeper.

The Barrier

The first thing to understand as a goalkeeper is that you must block the ball, be a barrier in its path to the goal. Then you can think about catching the ball.

Often, if you try to catch a hard shot or a slippery through ball, it will slide between your hands and either go into the net or fall in front of the goal. Use your hands to form a barrier at the moment of contact. In the basic block, your thumbs should be almost touching and your fingers up.

Try to catch the ball with your hands in this position. As you improve, you'll catch the ball most of the time. At the beginning, though, concentrate most on blocking the ball. If it drops to the ground, fall on it and smother it with your body.

The second barrier is your body, which should always be right behind the ball as you make a stop. If the ball squirts through your hands,

In rough-and-tumble play at Randall's Island Stadium, New York, in the fifties, a goalie comes out unhesitatingly to break up an attack. *Courtesy the National Soccer Hall of Fame at Oneonta, New York, Inc. John Albok*

it will then hit your chest or stomach and be blocked from getting away or going into the goal. Even the most routine save or stop should be made with your body squarely behind your hands.

Low Balls

There are two main ways of taking a ball that is moving on the ground toward you:

1. Standing with your feet together and your legs straight, blocking the path of the ball, lean over, hands palms up and side-by-side. Scoop the ball into your hands and pull it against your chest, cradling it with your arms.

To stop ground balls, stand with your feet together, scooping up the ball into your arms.

Drop to one knee, scooping up the ball and blocking the path to the goal with your foot and leg.

2. Going down on one knee, turn your kneeling leg perpendicular to the path of the ball so that there's no space between your knee and your other leg. Turn your upper body to face the ball and reach down to scoop it up as in the straight-leg pickup. Do not put your full weight on your knee, or you'll be unable to recover quickly if the ball takes a wrong bounce. Do not let your kneeling leg face forward, or the ball could hit your knee and bounce away.

Medium-Height Balls

Handle these shots as with the straight-leg scoop, and pull the ball into your midsection, giving a little as the ball comes in.

You can also catch the ball at chest level with your hands in the "W" position, fingers up and thumbs almost touching. Immediately pull the ball into your body and protect it with your arms.

A ball at medium level should be held at your midsection and protected with both arms and hands.

Catching High Balls

Do not be overanxious when going after a high ball coming into the goal area. Remember, you can use your hands while the other players have to jump to get to the ball with their heads. You can easily rise above them to catch the ball if you time your jump well. If you leave the ground too early, the ball might soar over your head.

Be sure to take a moment to judge the flight of the ball, marking which players are where and about to jump.

Go for the ball decisively and in one motion. Once you begin to go for any ball, high or low, do not hesitate. Shout to your teammates that you're coming and go. Preferably jump from a running start because that will give you more height and more power, should you collide with others in midair.

As you jump off one leg, bring your other leg up so your knee is out to protect you. Catch the ball at the highest point you can reach, and as you come down, pull it into your body to protect it.

Punching and Deflecting the Ball

In many cases you will not be able to catch a high ball. Perhaps too many players are around it; perhaps the ball is a slow, floating cross or just too high to pull down; or perhaps the shot comes too suddenly for you to grab the ball securely. In these situations you can punch the ball away or deflect it in another direction.

PUNCHING THE BALL: To punch a high ball that is straight ahead of you, go up with both fists pressed together. If you have time as you jump, make sure to raise that knee again to protect yourself. Meet the ball solidly with your fists, directing it more than punching it because it has plenty of force of its own that you use to send it away.

If you try to punch the ball like a boxer, you'll more easily miss it. Meet the ball with your entire body and direct it where you want it. In most cases, the easiest place to send the ball is straight back where it came from. In this way, you get the most powerful punch possible and are more certain of connecting fully with the ball.

On high shots that are almost out of reach, tip the ball over the bar, reaching with the arm opposite the shot and palming the ball out of play.

You can punch with one hand when you have no other choice, but learn with two hands and try to use both whenever possible. Of course, catching the ball is the best thing to do. Usually, if you can set two hands to the ball, then it's catchable.

TIPPING OVER THE BAR: When you find yourself with a high ball sailing toward the goal and out of catching reach, you can tip the ball over the cross-bar.

This deflection, too, uses the force of the ball to your advantage. With the palm and fingers of one hand, guide or flick the ball over the bar and out of play. If you are running backward and to your left, reach up with your right hand to deflect the ball, and vice versa.

The spectacular diving save is instinctive, but you must learn the technique by hard and frequent practice.

Again, be sure to block the ball before you try to catch it. Using the "W" form with your hands, reach for the ball as you dive. Leap sideways, pushing off your far leg and getting down as fast as possible. Do not just fall on the ball, but throw yourself down on it forcefully.

Break the impact of the fall by letting your body down in stages. Your near leg comes first, the outside of your foot touching the ground, followed by your shin, knee, hip, upper arm, and torso. This rocking movement as you land prevents jarring your body.

U.S. national team goalkeeper Tony Meola dives to save a shot as a Czechoslovakian attacker, right, rushes in during a 1990 World Cup match. U.S. fullback Desmond Armstrong, center, protects his goalie. *Courtesy the National Soccer Hall of Fame at Oneonta, New York, Inc. Ed Clough*

Don't put one hand down to break the fall. This limits your ability to reach the ball with your dive. If you have elbow and knee pads, and if you land with the rocking movement, you'll be protected as you dive.

As always, gather the ball immediately into your body in the next motion, rolling over to present your back to the field. Smother the ball by curling around it, your head tucked in. This protects you and the ball from an overeager attacker.

Tackling One-on-One

When a goalkeeper must charge an attacker to prevent a shot or to get the ball, it should be done aggressively and without hesitation.

When the attacker is breaking through for a shot, the goalie has no choice but to rush forward to block. By moving toward the attacker, the goalie cuts down the area of the goal the attacker can see. The closer the goalie is to the attacker, the more difficult it is to shoot a ball past the goalie into the net. The goalie should keep coming until either he collides with the attacker and/or the ball or the attacker takes the shot.

The goalie must not have second thoughts in the middle of the rush, or the attacker can shoot over the hesitant goalie's head. On the other hand, a smart goalie might throw a fake at the last moment to make the attacker pause, allowing the goalie to make the final few yards' rush at the ball.

When you slide into the attacker, do it on your side, arms and legs outstretched to screen the goal. If you are too late, the full blast of the shot can strike you hard. If your timing is right, the force of the kick can be almost eliminated by your simultaneous collision with the ball.

The first object of rushing out like this is to block a shot. The second is to hurry the attacker into making a mistake. Only third is to get your hands firmly on the ball. Usually this play, when successful, results in a loose ball that has deflected off the goalie's legs or arms.

In general, you should look for the opportunity to do one of three things.

1. Get to the ball first.
2. Get to the ball at the same time as the attacker.
3. Get to the ball just after the attacker makes contact.

In one-on-one situations, the goalie must come out fast, diving at the attacker's feet to block the shot and knock the ball away.

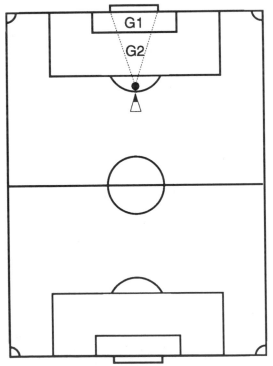

Cutting down the shooter's angle: The shooting angle, or area of goal visible to the shooter, is reduced as the goalkeeper comes off the goal line (G1) and moves into a position (G2) closer to the shooter and blocks the shot.

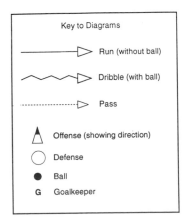

Key to Diagrams

———————▷ Run (without ball)

∿∿∿∿▷ Dribble (with ball)

- - - - - - ▷ Pass

△ Offense (showing direction)

○ Defense

● Ball

G Goalkeeper

If you cannot do any of these things, advance cautiously and stand your ground as the play develops.

After challenging, you must recover quickly, usually rushing at the loose ball again to clear or grab it. Seldom is it wise to run back into the goal immediately in the hope you'll have time to turn and save a shot. Once you're off the goal line, you'll have to stay out there until the ball is cleared or saved.

Your defenders should run into the goalmouth to back you up whenever you leave the line.

Take Your Time

Although there are many situations in which a swift and accurate throw or punt from a goalie can be an excellent offensive weapon, you must be sure, as goalie, to have the ball securely under control before trying to do anything with it. Take a moment to look around after catching the ball. This is no time for clumsiness or distraction. Waiting also allows your team to move out of the defense and get open for a pass. Your pause can take some of the wind out of the other team's sails, as they see a confident goalkeeper standing there coolly, not at all bothered by their offensive.

Looking around the field lets you pick where you want the ball to go and, more important, gets you in the habit of being sure to have a good grip on the ball after making the save.

As is true of every position, you should know what you are going to do with the ball before you catch it. Although you must not rush, the sooner you distribute the ball, the less chance your opponents have of figuring out the options for the offense.

Throwing

When playing goalie, teach yourself to throw for distance accurately, and your team will be assured of maintaining possession after you come up with the ball.

The long ball can be thrown overhand, like a football or baseball, if your hand is large enough to hold it. Otherwise, wrap your hand and

Showing perfect form, Milwaukee Wave goalkeeper Victor Nogueira sends the ball on the ground to a teammate during a National Professional Soccer League indoor game. *Courtesy NPSL*

wrist around the ball like a slingshot and whip it with a straight-arm delivery. Make the throw hard and low. A hanging ball comes down too slowly and gives the defense more time to intercept it. Always play to someone unmarked, who has time to trap it.

Faking to one player and throwing to another is a good practice that gives teammates a better chance of taking the ball down unchallenged.

The rolling, or bowling, style of throwing is effective for short distances. Get good speed on the ball so your teammate does not have to wait for it.

Punting and Dropkicking

The goalie's booming punt or long-carrying dropkick is a thing of beauty. Some soccer teams do not use long goalie kicks, preferring to pass and dribble the ball upfield. But most teams want that long kick as an effective method of starting an attack.

To punt, hold the ball at waist height, advance a few steps to build up steam, then drop the ball. When it is falling between your ankle and knee, kick it with your instep. Then follow through with your kicking foot, leaping forward and into the air to give more power.

The dropkick is similar, except that you kick the ball just as it strikes the ground, resulting in a lower trajectory and more speed. Strike the ball dead center and kick straight ahead rather than upward. The follow-through is the same.

In both kicks, accuracy should be developed along with power.

Goalie Conditioning

The goalie should do running and calisthenics along with teammates, adding extra exercises to strengthen the upper body and improve jumping ability.

Condition your upper body with push-ups, sit-ups, and moderate weight lifting, developing strength, not bulk. Jumping with ankle weights and skipping rope develops leaping ability.

Before you work out with the ball—and especially before trying to make saves, even easy ones—be sure to warm up, loosen muscles well, and stretch. When you are ready, kneel behind the goal and roll a ball to a teammate, who kicks it back first-time. Make relaxed saves and get the feeling of diving from this kneeling position before standing up to make more difficult saves.

In one effective drill that teaches reflexes as well as working on conditioning, the goalie lies down, facing the goal, and a teammate kicks or throws a ball at the goal, yelling, "Turn!" The goalie must get up while turning, then find the ball and make the save. In this drill, be sure you do not always turn to the same, or "favorite," side.

U.S. national team goalkeeper Tony Meola, here punching the ball away, achieved world-class status for his play in the years between the World Cup tournaments of 1990 and 1994. *Ed Clough*

Realistic Practices

A goalie who wants to practice is always welcome on a soccer field, because everyone else is eager to shoot on goal.

Make your workouts as close to game situations as possible. Don't be lazy, and never let the ball go in because you don't feel like diving for it. Get in the habit of going for every ball, whether it's savable or not. Develop the sense of cutting off the shooter's angle, and remind yourself to stand close to the near post when the shooter is coming from the side.

If you want to be a goalie, the never-give-up attitude should click on whenever you practice between the posts. Goalie is first a state of mind, second a soccer position.

 POINTS TO REMEMBER

- Learn to play soccer in the field while you also learn to be a goalie.
- The penalty box is your domain, and your teammates must get out of your way when you call them off.
- Be a barrier between the ball and the goal first; then try to catch the ball.
- Act decisively when you go for the ball. Don't stop until it's in your hands.
- Hold the ball securely while you decide what you'll do with it.

12 THE AMERICAN GAME YESTERDAY AND TODAY

Not so very long ago, soccer balls weren't bouncing all over America.

Before 1967 it was unusual to see a soccer field anywhere, especially in the suburbs or out in the country. Generally, any field that soccer enthusiasts did find had grimy sticks for goals, no nets, and faded wiggly sidelines running partway up a slope. Nothing glamorous, but it was a soccer field, and soccer lovers craned their necks as they drove past, wondering who played there and how good they were.

That's all changed.

Today, soccer fields are everywhere in America, especially on suburban high school campuses, and they've never looked so good. In many cases the goals stay up all year, because there might be half a dozen youth games on weekends throughout the spring and summer. The boom of youth-club soccer has changed the face of American parks and athletic complexes.

Even more impressive than school facilities are new soccer centers with five or ten fields. These are often owned by youth clubs or by town recreation departments, but soccer complexes and indoor arenas are also being built as business ventures.

It has been said that the United States has no soccer tradition, but history proves otherwise. For almost four centuries the game has been played in America, though in various forms.

Near Plymouth in 1620 sea-weary English Pilgrims found Indians playing their own version of "foot balle" with a deerskin ball on the beaches. As the years passed, European colonists arrived with their own ways of playing the ancient game of "foot ball," a term that means playing with a ball on foot rather than on horseback. So *voetbal, futebol, fútbol,* and *ballon* came to North America, eventually to develop into the modern sport that only Americans now call soccer.

There was nothing glamorous about New York's soccer fields in the fifties, but play could be thrilling, as shown in this photo at a game in Brooklyn. *Courtesy the National Soccer Hall of Fame at Oneonta, New York, Inc. John Albok*

On Boston Common in the 1860s, schoolboys played football according to the newly written rules of "association football." In 1869 the first intercollegiate "football" game was played, with Rutgers beating Princeton. This game was destined to be popularly noted as the first authentic intercollegiate "American football" game, but the rules were those of association football, or soccer. Ivy League colleges decided to play football with the rules of rugby rather than soccer in 1876.

College soccer vanished from the American scene until after the turn of the century, but soccer continued to be played elsewhere. Hundreds of factories had their own teams, which were formed into leagues. In 1884 the American Football Association was established in Newark, New Jersey, the first major semiprofessional soccer organization. The first semipro soccer league was formed the following year in Fall River, Massachusetts.

In 1894 the eastern teams of the National Baseball League organized the first professional soccer league in the United States. The pur-

Billy Gonsalves, a native of Fall River, Massachusetts, scored more than 1,000 goals in his career and is considered one of the best Americans ever to play the game. *Courtesy the National Soccer Hall of Fame at Oneonta, New York, Inc. John Albok*

pose was to draw fans to the empty stadiums during the fall-winter season. Teams carried the names of the baseball clubs—including the New York Giants, Washington Senators, and Baltimore Orioles.

Halfhearted promotion and poor management doomed the league; matches conflicted with baseball and college football games. After one season, these fields of soccer dreams were shut down by the baseball owners.

In the fifty-year period between 1880 and the depression of the thirties, more than 27 million immigrants entered the United States. Their native game was soccer. Many lost interest in the game, considering it "foreign," and along with it they dropped their names, their cultures, and their mother tongues. But others kept playing.

Haverford College in Haverford, Pennsylvania, started a soccer team in 1902, led by student Richard M. Gummere, a native of England. Playing against teams sponsored by local cricket clubs and high schools, Haverford initiated modern collegiate soccer. Gummere went on to Harvard, where two years later he helped revive association football. In a pair of Harvard defeats against Haverford, intercollegiate soccer competition officially began. California had college teams at Stanford and Berkeley by 1910, and with more colleges establishing teams, a nascent movement was under way.

In 1904 soccer was played for the first time in the Olympics—held in St. Louis that year—with clubs, not national teams, competing. American clubs competed, but the Canadians won.

In 1905, encouraged by President Teddy Roosevelt's call for an alternative to the violence and mayhem of "American football," a group of English amateur players was invited by American soccer interests to tour the United States and Canada. The team put on a devastating exhibition, defeating almost everyone in sight. During the tour soccer attendance records were broken everywhere, with 44,000 at a game in the Polo Grounds in New York City. This skillful all-star team called itself, coincidentally, the Pilgrims.

The U.S. Soccer Federation was established in 1913 in the hope that a major professional soccer league could be sustained. In the years leading to and after World War I, native-born American players came into their own.

Through the twenties U.S. soccer was dominated by American-born players, but abroad the game had developed much faster with profes-

The 1950 U.S. national team that defeated England 1–0 in World Cup play in Brazil, coached by Bill Jeffrey, back row, right. *Courtesy the National Soccer Hall of Fame at Oneonta, New York, Inc.*

sional leagues. Some new immigrants to America were former pros, and their expertise elevated the level of American soccer.

Established in 1930, the first World Cup tournament was played in Uruguay, with the best teams attending by invitation. The United States reached the semifinals, defeating Belgium and Paraguay to get there. Most of the players on this team were American-born. Among them was high-scoring Billy Gonsalves of Fall River, Massachusetts, regarded as the finest player of the thirties and sometimes called "the Babe Ruth of American soccer."

In the 1934 tournament the United States was defeated 7–1 by Italy, the eventual champion. To get to the tournament the United States defeated Mexico, and Buff Donelli set a World Cup record by scoring four goals in the game.

The volatile prewar year 1938 saw many nations decline to play in the French World Cup, in which the United States was knocked out early. There was no tournament during the war and postwar years. In 1950 the World Cup was held in Brazil, where the U.S. team staged a stunning 1–0 upset of the English. Then considered the best team in the world, the English were utterly humiliated.

With the new influx of immigrants after World War II, soccer in America was again branded "foreign" and seemed doomed to remain a minor sport, in terms of both participation and spectators. Ethnic clubs became the focus of the best soccer, but colleges and high schools that played the game were growing in number and in quality.

By the seventies, following the enormous worldwide broadcast audience for the 1966 World Cup, American entrepreneurs began to develop a major professional soccer league.

Pelé and the Cosmos and the North American Soccer League (NASL)

The American media never paid much attention to soccer until 1975, when the great and charismatic Pelé, Brazil's "national treasure," joined the North American Soccer League's New York Cosmos and stimulated a tremendous youth movement that exploded throughout the seventies. At the time, the NASL was the sole survivor of several short-lived, high-budget attempts to get a truly professional soccer league off the ground in the United States.

NASL marketers believed that to bring in the crowds they had to present "good soccer," as played by world-class athletes. So NASL clubs spent millions for players. Pelé made a worldwide sensation by coming out of retirement to join the Cosmos. He had been offered a blank check to play in Mexico, but chose the Cosmos instead because he felt he had a mission to popularize soccer in the United States. He succeeded.

The Cosmos soon became international celebrities and quickly grew into one of the finest and highest-paid teams in the world. Pelé was joined on the Cosmos by some of the greatest names the modern game has known: West Germany's Franz Beckenbauer, Italy's Giorgio Chinaglia, Brazil's Carlos Alberto, and Russia's Erol Yasin. During his three years with the Cosmos, Pelé filled stadium after stadium, well earning the $4.5 million he was paid. His charisma and talent caught the imagination of American youngsters, and youth soccer took off. Crowds of

In the mid-seventies Brazilian star Pelé brought his international reputation and brilliant skills to the New York Cosmos of the North American Soccer League, sparking American children's interest in soccer as never before. *Courtesy the National Soccer Hall of Fame at Oneonta, New York, Inc.*

50,000 were common wherever Pelé went with the Cosmos. The American media was caught up in the excitement and for a time closely followed the Cosmos and the league.

Other NASL clubs acquired fading superstars like Ireland's George Best, Portugal's Eusebio, Holland's Johann Cruyff, and England's Bobby Moore. NASL soccer rocketed to the top of the popularity charts in almost every regional market in the United States and Canada. The Portland Timbers, Tampa Bay Rowdies, Chicago Sting, and Dallas Toronado became the favorite names of teams in mushrooming youth soccer leagues.

Glittering soccer stardust was sprinkled freely and expensively on the playing fields of the NASL. World-famous players competed alongside fine young American athletes like Kyle Rote, Jr., Jeff Durgan, Ricky Davis, Bob Rigby, and Werner Roth. And these American players became legitimate stars—in 1973 Rote led the league in scoring and Rigby in goals-allowed percentage. That same year, Rote won ABC television's "Superstars" competition against the greatest professional athletes in the country.

By the time Pelé finally retired in 1977, bidding an emotional farewell to more than 77,000 soccer fans in Giants Stadium, it looked as if pro soccer really had come of age in America.

But in a few years the flash and glitter faded. No other clubs in the NASL had the resources of the Cosmos, whose coup in bringing in Pelé was a publicity-grabber impossible to top. Although NASL soccer was excellent, fan loyalty still had not been won by enough NASL clubs. Kids interested in the game were too busy playing on newly formed youth teams on Sundays to watch the NASL teams. Also, ethnic players and fans cared more about their own clubs and did not support the big-time NASL pros. Without the show-biz aura of the seventies, the American media settled back into its studied ignorance of—and often hostility to—soccer.

The NASL lost momentum, and club owners, unable to win television contracts, lost money. In 1984, although on the verge of folding, the teams of the NASL played fifteen games against some of the best professional squads in the world, including the reigning World Cup champion, Italy, and the league champions from Germany and Brazil. The result was an astonishing 13-1-1 in the NASL's favor.

But the club owners were tired of losing money, and the NASL, with a couple of the best teams in the world, crashed in 1984. Some NASL clubs are still in operation today, playing in smaller, semipro leagues that struggle on in the hope that the 1994 World Cup will give the game another mighty boost and lay the foundation for a permanent professional league.

Soccer on Sunday

Back in 1967, what few permanent soccer fields there were outside of colleges usually belonged to the German Americans or the Greek Americans or the Scots-Americans—the "ethnic clubs." These fields were usually scrubby and stony because they were hard used for Sunday games and practice several nights a week, sometimes until eleven P.M. under dim floodlights.

Part of an American tradition that reaches back to nineteenth-century immigrants and milltown teams sponsored by factories, ethnic-club soccer still thrives. The games are played on Sundays, rain or shine or blizzard.

In some ways fan enthusiasm for local ethnic club soccer on Sunday aided the demise of the NASL. A fan of the Maccabee Sport Club in Los Angeles probably cared more about a league game between his or her local team and the L.A. Kickers than about an NASL Aztec game. Fans went to local club games because they liked the Union Lancers, because they wanted to see their friends on the Newark Ukrainians or Latino Americano. That loyalty is a cornerstone of ethnic-club soccer. *Fan identification* is the marketing term for it, and few NASL clubs were ever able to bottle it. For a few years of fleeting glory the NASL came close to succeeding, but the enormous expense involved in presenting "good soccer"—as played by the best players in the world—made the clubs unprofitable. Most owners, understandably, gave up.

American Soccer Today

The NASL's lost momentum did not mean lost momentum for soccer in the United States. On the contrary, all that sacrifice and work, all that investment in time and money and marketing, had made a mighty breakthrough, though that breakthrough did not fill the stands at NASL games.

Americans were busy playing the game themselves, kicking a ball with their kids in parks and backyards, or playing on high school and college teams, on youth teams, on new clubs that had not existed a couple of years before. By 1984, 8 million Americans were playing soccer and loving it. The Olympic Games that year in Los Angeles further captured the imagination of American fans. Just as in Montreal a few years earlier, soccer outdrew all the other Olympic sports combined; two games in the Rose Bowl drew more than 100,000 fans each. Through the rest of the eighties, soccer fully blossomed as a youth sport as former "Pelé children" of the sixties and seventies passed along their love of the game to their kids.

Women's collegiate play in matches like this between Columbia and Rutgers has developed a high level of soccer ability, making the women's national team one of the best in the world.   *Cynthia Greer*

Women's soccer was also taking off in the eighties. Just a decade before, girls' and women's soccer was scarcely thought of, and the few females who came to ethnic-club games sat at tables in the restaurant, out of earshot of the men's rough talk. Today, of the more than 15 million Americans who play soccer, 6 million are girls or young women, with the finest athletes competing at the scholastic and collegiate levels. Women's soccer in the United States has developed swiftly into one of the strongest programs in the world.

Professional indoor soccer leagues won some television coverage and local fan support in the eighties. Several semipro leagues struggled to become one North American league, but a stable professional soccer league was not yet established.

In 1990 the U.S. men's national team, made up largely of players with little more than college-level experience, qualified for the World Cup in Italy. Though young and inexperienced, the team almost tied Italy and won the affection of foreign fans everywhere for its courage and effort.

Meanwhile, the women's national team steamrollered its way to the first-ever Women's World Cup, held in China in 1991. Not only did they win the cup, they routed almost every team they played, putting on a remarkable exhibition of athletic ability and soccer skill. Around the world American women players were admired for their outstanding athletic and soccer abilities.

Youth Soccer: Twenty-five Years of Swift Growth

Back in the sixties, when most Americans had never seen a soccer game, more colleges had soccer teams than had football teams, and organized collegiate squads had been playing the game enthusiastically since the turn of the century. Still, soccer was looked at as something foreign, or preppy, by most Americans. That view changed quickly, however, with the youth soccer boom of the seventies, and by 1993 soccer was the second-most-popular youth participation sport in the United States. Almost 12 million under the age of eighteen played some soccer in 1993, about 6 million in youth leagues. Only basketball, with 18 million participants, had more kids involved. In 1989 there were 180,000 registered soccer teams; in 1993 there were 200,000; and the youth movement is still gaining momentum, with the United States Youth Soccer Association (USYSA, a branch of the United States Soccer Federation, the national governing body) registering 1.9 million players.

Today, just as most fans come to ethnic-club games because friends and relatives are playing, millions of American parents, who know little about soccer, come to cheer for their children in the youth and scholastic leagues. And by now, Sunday soccer on the fields of the ethnic clubs is more American than ever because of the growing number of talented homegrown players.

Children in Chatham, New York, play a recreation league game with small goals.

Of all the soccer associations in the United States that have worked hard to bring soccer to children, none is more successful than the California-based American Youth Soccer Organization (AYSO). Founded in 1964, before the boom years of youth soccer, AYSO is unique among the world's youth soccer associations because its first rule is that every child must play at least half the game. Teaching youngsters good sportsmanship is first and foremost for AYSO, and soccer is a means to that goal.

AYSO's second rule is that teams in a league must be balanced according to ability. Rule three opens registration equally to boys and girls—a revolutionary idea in the seventies. The fourth and key rule is that coaching must always be positive. AYSO has a "Bill of Rights for Young Athletes" and a code of behavior for players, coaches, and parents called "Be a Good Sport" (see Appendix B).

AYSO has maintained its philosophy even during recent years of extremely rapid growth. Many members would have liked to run soccer programs in the more traditional way: First play to win, and let players with lesser ability ride the bench. However, AYSO does not bend its guiding principles. From the start it has stressed healthy competition, accentuating respect for opponents and officials. AYSO also formally demands that its "regions," as local groups are called, make sure coaches and parent volunteers are positive role models.

AYSO volunteers are more than moms with bags of sliced oranges for halftime and dads chauffeuring players back and forth. They include as many as 40,000 volunteer coaches, who regularly take AYSO instructional courses, and 15,000 unpaid referees, who are required to attend clinics and camps sponsored by AYSO. Getting enough referees, even paid ones, is the toughest part of running any local league, but AYSO has overcome this problem by growing its own.

In this spirit the organization has established more than 720 regions in 43 states. In 1993 there were more than 430,000 children on 35,000 AYSO teams, with 175,000 adult coaches, referees, and volunteers. In 1984 AYSO volunteers helped run the Los Angeles Olympics. With growth came international travel and tournaments with visiting foreign youth teams.

Through the years, the everyone-plays philosophy, balanced teams, and positive coaching have been the cornerstones of AYSO success. As proof the organization knows what it's doing, a recent survey of children who play soccer found that 78 percent would rather play regularly on a team that loses than ride the bench on a team that wins.

World Cup USA '94

Although the officials of international games recognized the growth of American soccer, the world soccer community was surprised on July 4, 1988, when the United States was awarded the prestigious World Cup tournament for 1994. Why choose the United States for this greatest single-sport spectacle in the world? How could FIFA (Fédération Internationale de Football Association) give the World Cup to a country where the sport is run mostly by volunteers, played by amateurs, and looked upon by the American mass media as a minor sport?

The answer is that American youth soccer is the largest, richest, and best-organized youth soccer movement in the world. FIFA administrators gambled, withstanding widespread criticism from high-pressure, high-finance foreign club owners, when it selected a country without a major pro league for the World Cup tournament. Another reason they chose the United States is that this is the last great market not completely won over by soccer, and there are millions more young potential players here.

1984: NASL VERSUS THE WORLD

Proof that the North American Soccer League was world class is seen on this chart of international games played in 1984 by NASL clubs or mainly NASL players.

The record is 13 wins, 1 loss, 1 tie.

Date	Team		Opponent		Site
5/28	Cosmos	5	Barcelona, Spain	3	Meadowlands
5/30	Team America	0	Italian National	0	Meadowlands
5/30	Toronto	1	Udinese, Italy	0	Toronto
6/2	U.S. Olympic	2	Stuttgart, Germany	3	St. Louis
6/3	Cosmos	4	Udinese, Italy	1	Meadowlands
6/6	Tampa Bay	3	Stuttgart, Germany	2	Tampa
6/6	Vancouver	3	Fulminese, Brazil	1	Vancouver
6/8	Vancouver	3	Stuttgart, Germany	1	Vancouver
6/10	Golden Bay	4	Stuttgart, Germany	2	San Jose
6/13	Tampa Bay	1	Hull City, England	0	Tampa
6/13	Minnesota	5	Glasgow Rangers	2	Minneapolis
6/13	Toronto	2	Stuttgart, Germany	0	Toronto
6/15	Toronto	2	Glasgow Rangers	0	Toronto
6/16	Tampa Bay	3	Stoke City, England	1	Tampa
6/17	Golden Bay	2	Sporting Lisbon	1	San Jose

NOTES: The Italian national team was the reigning world champion that year. Stuttgart was the champion of the West German Bundesliga. Fulminese was the Brazilian national champion.

Compiled by Samuel Foulds, historian of the United States Soccer Federation.

Today, instead of a few lonely balls aloft at ethnic-club fields on Sundays, American skies are filled with soccer balls. And on Saturdays, too, when some youth organizations such as AYSO prefer to play. Children are scampering about in colorful uniforms, on teams with names like Pleasant Valley Cosmos, Chatham Strikers, Middletown Sting, and Centerville Kicks. Their parents probably don't know where those team names came from, and very few have any idea what "good soccer" is, but it doesn't matter, because to most of them "good" is what's good for their kids.

Now soccer is everywhere in the United States, thanks to those semipro club players who for a century kept American soccer alive, and thanks to the college teams that taught soccer to generations of young athletes who passed their love of the game down to their children.

And thanks to the pioneering NASL, which packed stadiums with cheering kids who saw close up the world's finest soccer players of the seventies and eighties. Today, those kids are parents, and they remember the great Pelé, who shared with them his love for what he calls "the beautiful game."

13 TO THE AMERICAN SPECTATOR LEARNING ABOUT SOCCER

At the heart of soccer is the fun of kicking a bouncing ball. Add an opponent or two, a teammate, goals made of shirts laid on the ground, and fun becomes a game. With full teams, colorful uniforms, a grassy field, big white goalposts and nets, cheering fans, and something to win or lose for, the game becomes sport, pageantry, and passion.

Body contact is rough, attacks and counterattacks are thrilling, and the ball is constantly moving. Action is fast, goal-scoring a rush of glory and despair. Playing soccer is excitement and fun—being a soccer spectator, however, is something else altogether.

Young People Need Youthful Soccer

For those who are unfamiliar with soccer, it's important to keep in mind that what youngsters are doing—or should be doing—is far different from what professionals are doing.

Not every coach or player realizes that. Often American children are indoctrinated by coaches who understand only "competitive soccer."

American national team players celebrate their 1—0 victory over
Trinidad and Tobago, which qualified them for Italia '90.
Jon Van Woerden

Such coaches usually did not learn the game until they were teenagers,
and then only in a structured situation.

Generally, these overorganized coaches did not play soccer with
friends or family as children, and they do not really understand the joy
of playing. Their players are constantly overseen by coaches and referees, and they do one drill after another, playing too many full-field
scrimmages with large goals. Such coaches are often too serious, and

as a result their players and the parents of their players become too serious.

Their teams learn short passing until it comes out of their ears. They grimly drill as the coach serves the ball. They become used to shooting once at the goal and then stumping to the back of a long line to await their turns to shoot again. They seldom play small-sided games, and they never try to dribble.

If the other teams in the league are not familiar with soccer, the drilled and overorganized often win more than they lose. This convinces players and parents that the coach's regimented system is good. Unfortunately, the players do not become good soccer players, and they seldom play the game after high school.

On the other hand, the coach who played as a child will usually impart a love of soccer to young players. Practices will involve a lot of games in small groups. Players won't be afraid to make mistakes, and the coach will encourage them to dribble as often as possible.

No child will become good at soccer if all he learns is how to pass the ball every time it comes his way. The old adage "A pass is better than a dribble" may be right much of the time at the higher levels of soccer, but at the organized youth level it is essential that the coach get out of the way and let the kids play.

Play "Keepaway"

In my childhood there were fifty kids and one ball on a Scottish school yard. "Keepaway" was the game, and that was how we learned to "play" and to dribble, like kids playing American football's "kill the man with the ball." No coach or parent came out to tell us to pass. What fun is passing in school-yard soccer?

Thirty years later, as a high school coach in rural upstate New York, I would set up two teams and two goals on a half-field and then toss a ball out, saying to the players, "No passing allowed. And no shooting. You can only score by dribbling into the goal."

At first the players were startled, but after a little while their soccer attitudes changed. Soon they all became dribblers, and they had a lot of fun as their understanding of the game opened up.

Kids Play Naturally

Winning games at the juvenile soccer level is not as important as letting the kids play naturally, with a minimum of organized drills. Yes, teach them positional play, but don't overdo it. Teach them to pass, but encourage them to dribble when they think it's the right time. And let them understand that they're not ball hogs just because they do so.

There's a right time for passing and a right time for holding the ball. No coach can teach that; it has to be learned at a young age.

As you watch children up to age twelve play soccer, whether organized or just pickup, pay attention to how much they dribble. You'll come to know when players are holding the ball too long, when they should pass or shoot, and you'll come to appreciate the good dribblers instead of thinking that all dribblers are doing the wrong thing.

And when it comes to judging youth coaches, you'll know how "good" they are by listening to the laughter on the practice field. The more the better.

Older Levels of Soccer

If you've come to appreciate the joy of children playing soccer, you'll better appreciate the discipline and skill and courage of good soccer players at older age levels.

Here you'll see less dribbling and more passing. You can judge the quality of the play by how effectively a team moves the ball. Decisive, skillful passing gets the ball in front of the goal for a shot.

Here you also come to appreciate the athleticism of players who may not have such great skills but who perform with excitement and inspiration on the field. Of course, if you care who wins or loses, the game is more appealing than ever. And if you have a youngster playing, you'll find that your understanding of the game will change as your child plays different positions.

Expect the coach to be positive and encouraging. Good sportsmanship is more essential than ever; otherwise young athletes never learn how to lose—or how to win. Listen to the coach under the pressure of a game situation, and you'll soon know how the players are being taught.

The non-soccer-playing American parent should not suspend what

Since 1975 American children have made soccer one of their favorite sports, playing both in organized youth leagues and in pickup games.

he or she has learned about right and wrong in athletics when it comes to watching soccer. Bring your highest standards to the experience and demand, above all, that your child has fun, win or lose.

There's little you can do about a coach you don't like, but you must continue to encourage your child to play to the highest standards of soccer and sportsmanship. Part of the athlete's long-term experience is playing for coaches who have low standards or who are too bent on winning at any cost.

If parents support and encourage their young soccer player, the athlete will make the best of every difficult situation. Do not criticize the coach behind his or her back, but explain to your child that being on the team requires teamwork, and that includes trying to find the best in what the coach is teaching.

At Higher Levels of Soccer

At the professional, semiprofessional, and collegiate levels, the soccer is at its most skillful, even when played defensively. Now you're watching a spectacle, where good sportsmanship shines more brilliantly and where bad sportsmanship is at its most vicious. For professionals, every game is life or death, honor or shame.

Professional soccer is fascinating to spectators who are familiar with the players or with the story behind the teams. To really appreciate the highest levels of soccer, you have to know the teams and care who wins. Then, when a team plays defensively, slowing the game down in order just to tie, for instance, you'll understand why and be thrilled by the players' skill.

Watching Good Soccer

As you watch topflight soccer, try to scan the entire field, not watching only the player with the ball. See how the players without the ball move, cutting to get open or playing tight defense.

Let your eye go from the ball handler to nearby teammates and guess what will happen next. Watch the players constantly trying to outwit each other, trying to break clear for a pass, or working to keep an opponent from getting clear.

When a team is advancing on goal, watch how the attackers move and how the defenders respond. Watch the goalkeeper before he leaps to save a shot or moves out to smother a breakaway. Anticipate. Look around, as we say on the soccer field, and you as the spectator will appreciate the game far better than you would by focusing only on the ball.

The Officials

The referee's task is to keep the game under control, but with as little stoppage as possible. Above all, the referee must be consistent—not necessarily exactly right in rules interpretation, but consistent so that both teams know what to expect.

One of the fastest ways for a referee to lose control of a game and enrage the players is to make different judgment calls on the same infraction. For example, a referee who first permits a player who has been fouled to keep on going with the ball—the "advantage" rule—must be sure to make the same judgment call when the other team is fouled.

The referee must be consistent as well as fair. Most experienced coaches would rather work with a mediocre referee who calls fairly and consistently than with a knowledgeable but unpredictable one.

The best officials take no lip from any player or coach and warn everyone about this before the game starts. Flashing a yellow card of caution or a red card of expulsion is a last resort for a referee. It is best if competitors are strictly silenced by the ref at the very first outbreak of ill temper. A good ref will give players some latitude, taking emotions into consideration, but everyone on the soccer field knows when the line of disrespect has been crossed.

You'll recognize a good referee right from the start: The whistle is sharp and loud, the voice and commands decisive. In many a big-time game there is a moment early on when the referee briefly stops play to pointedly address an overexcited or intentionally dirty player. No yellow flag is waved, and there's no yelling. But everyone knows this referee means business. From then on, the referee sets the pace of the game, controls the amount of time taken in throw-ins and free kicks. The referee will ignore most dirty looks, but after fair warning the first open insult from a player or coach will be answered with a yellow card. As with every call, the "booking" is done unemotionally and without permitting argument.

If you're a parent interested in really understanding soccer, read up on the rules and learn what you can, then offer to officiate a practice scrimmage for your child's youth team. You'll never forget it. One day you'll find yourself watching a high-level soccer match and admiring the referee as much as the players. Maybe more.

Learning Soccer Yourself

If you're an adult who wants to learn the game, the best way is to play in the backyard or in the park with kids. Start with small children so you don't get hurt. Be sure to wear good sneakers that protect your toes, and be careful not to kick anyone or hit anyone with the ball in your enthusiasm. Try playing "keepaway."

People who criticize soccer have never played it for fun. And if you don't first play it for fun—whether you're young or old—you'll never learn how to play soccer at all. At the heart of soccer is the fun of kicking a bouncing ball, and a ball is all you need.

Only after you've once kicked a soccer ball for fun are you ready to be a spectator.

14 THE LAWS OF THE GAME

All over the world, soccer rules are standardized, established by the Fédération Internationale de Football Association (FIFA) and implemented consistently in each country by one regulatory body—except in the United States.

In the United States there are several regulatory bodies for sports, and soccer rules are different from one regulatory organization to another. College, secondary school, professional, amateur, and youth soccer in the United States all have rules that differ slightly from FIFA's international laws of the game.

For example, more substitutes are allowed by American rules than by FIFA rules, which permit only three, with players not permitted to return to the game. In secondary school soccer, substitution is unlimited, with players moving in and out at the coach's discretion.

Another difference is that FIFA rules call for one referee and two linesmen, while college and scholastic soccer employ two referees and no linesmen. FIFA allows five minutes between halves; colleges and secondary schools allow ten.

There are other minor differences between collegiate and scholastic—such as how uniforms are numbered, whether protective devices such as casts may be worn, and the length and composition of studs on shoes. College and scholastic soccer forbids jewelry and restricts hair length, but professionals can wear what they want as long as it is not hazardous.

One of the most glaring differences is seen in the battle jumping for head balls. Some scholastic leagues forbid the defender to lean over the attacker to get to the ball, while FIFA rules permit this move—indeed, you often can't win a ball in the air without doing it—as long as the defender does not foul the attacker.

For the most part, however, the laws of soccer are pretty much the same around the world. Some rules are changing and unsettled, with experimentation going on in various countries under FIFA supervision. Rules under question include how long a goalkeeper may hold the ball, whether the goal should be slightly wider, and how the offsides rule might be changed.

The Field of Play

The soccer field is rectangular, its length between 100 and 130 yards, its width between 50 and 100 yards. For youth soccer, under age sixteen, the dimensions are smaller, the length no more than 100 yards and the width proportionally narrower.

The penalty box—or penalty area or goal area—is in front of the goal and extends eighteen yards into the field and thirty-six yards across the face of the goal. This dimension should be altered in proportion to the overall dimensions of the field, which can be laid out according to space limitations or the age of the players.

The goals are twenty-four feet wide by eight feet high for senior games, but proportionally smaller for youth soccer on smaller fields.

Likewise, the ball comes in several sizes, with "5" being the largest, the one used in senior soccer, and smaller sizes for children. (For decades Brazil has been known for using a slightly smaller ball in professional play, making it harder for visiting foreign teams to compete.)

When organizing youth soccer, it's crucial to create smaller fields and use balls that are the right size for the age group, so the children

THE SOCCER FIELD

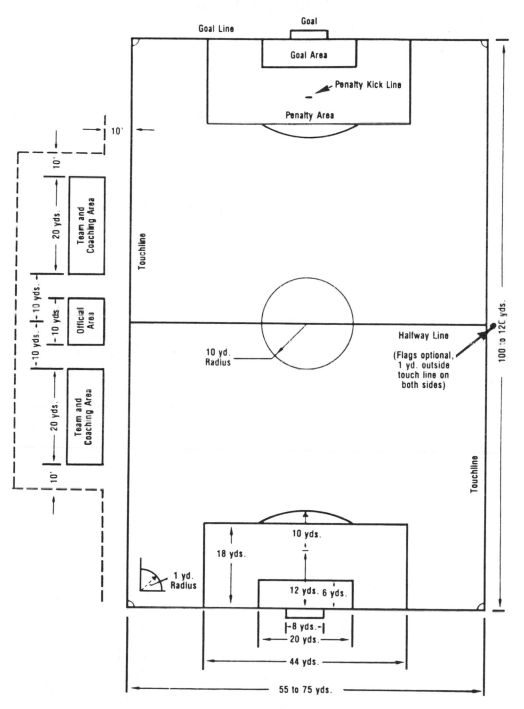

can kick well, without injury to tender knees. The kids should also be able to get the smaller ball up and down the field to score goals. Young children often want to play on full-size fields with full-size balls at first, but give them the experience of playing with the right ball on the right field for their age, and they'll soon realize how much more fun it is.

The Teams

Eleven players make up a team. The goalkeeper is the only player permitted to use his hands, and then only in the penalty box and under limited circumstances, the rules for which are currently changing from season to season and league to league. In most cases the goalie may take only three steps while holding the ball. He may not in one play catch a ball, drop it, and pick it up again. (This infraction gives an indirect kick to the other team.) Nor may the goalie pick up a ball intentionally kicked back by a teammate; he must play it with his feet like a field player.

Any player may change places (and uniforms) with the goalkeeper at a stoppage in play (i.e., a goal, a referee card warning, a penalty kick, a drop ball, a period break such as halftime) as long as the referee is informed before the exchange is made.

Any substitution must first be approved by the referee. In scholastic and college games, substitution during the run of play can only be made at a throw-in (your own possession), at a corner kick (your own possession), or at any goal kick. Substitution can also be made at any stoppage in play.

Player Equipment

Equipment regulations vary from country to country and league to league, but in general no player may wear anything that can injure another player or himself. Shoes, for instance, may not have dangerously long studs.

The goalkeeper must wear colors that distinguish him from other players and from the referee. Generally, collegiate and scholastic teams are required to have home and away uniforms; lighter-color jerseys are worn with lighter-color socks, and darker with darker.

The Length of the Game

A standard soccer game consists of two periods of forty-five minutes each, unless otherwise agreed upon by both teams. The clock stops only under the direction of the referee or after a score. There are no time-outs. The referee extends time to make up for "injury time" used up during delays of the game.

Youth and scholastic leagues reduce the length of the game—under age fourteen usually has thirty-five-minute halves and under age sixteen has forty-minute halves—and sometimes youth games are played in quarters. Other soccer games, such as indoor and five-a-side, have their own regulations.

The Kickoff

After team captains toss a coin to decide who chooses either goal to defend or ball possession, the game begins with each team lining up in its own half of the field. The kickoff is taken at the center circle, and all defenders must stand outside this circle until the ball is played. The kicker may not touch the ball again until another player touches it first.

At the referee's whistle to start the game, the ball must be sent forward with the kickoff and must travel at least its circumference before it may be touched by another player. If the kickoff is improper, it is taken again. Offensive players must remain in their own half of the field until the ball is kicked.

Ball In and out of Play

One of the most controversial judgment calls is whether the ball has gone far enough across a line to be considered a goal or out-of-bounds. The ball is out of play when it has wholly crossed the goal line or sideline, whether in the air or on the ground. It's not a goal unless it crosses the goal line completely.

Offsides

A player is in an offsides position if he is nearer than the ball to the opponent's goal line, unless

    1. The player is in his own half of the field of play.

    2. There are at least two opponents nearer than the player to their own goal line.

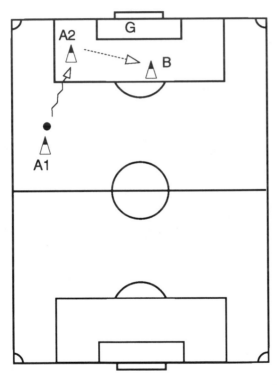

Not offsides: The attacker dribbles the ball from A1 to the A2 position and then passes to teammate B, who is not offsides because the ball is ahead of B at the moment it is passed.

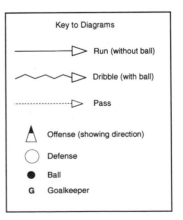

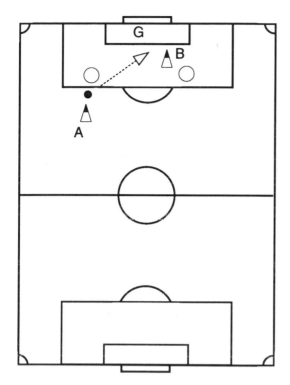

Offsides: B is offsides at the moment the ball is passed because there is only one defender (the goalie) between B and the goal.

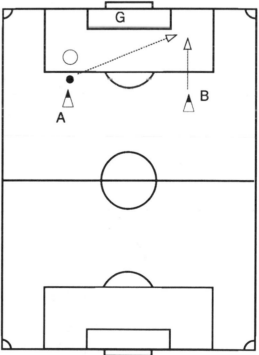

Not offsides: B is not offsides because at the moment A passes the ball there are two defenders between B and the goal.

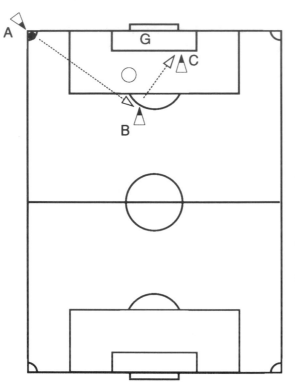

Offsides: C is offsides after this corner kick is taken, because there are not at least two defenders between him and the goal at the moment B passes the ball.

A player is not offsides if he is standing even with the second-to-last defender.

A player can be declared offsides only if, at the moment the ball touches or is played by one of the player's team, he is

1. Interfering with play or an opponent.
2. Seeking to gain advantage by being in that position.

A player is not offsides if he is directly receiving a ball from a goal kick, a corner kick, a throw-in, or a drop ball.

A player will not automatically be declared offsides just because he is in an offsides position. This is a judgment call by the referee, who must decide whether the offsides position influences the developing play.

For example, an attacker who is offsides in a wide position while the play is taking place right in front of the goal might not be called offsides. If the goalie or a defender has to take that attacker into account during the play, then the attacker is offsides.

Obviously, controversy develops when the referee's judgment of offsides does not agree with everyone else's. In the heat of swift action close to the goal, it is difficult to see who is onsides and who is not.

Fouls and Misconduct

A *direct free kick* is awarded for the following infractions:

1. Kicking or attempting to kick an opponent.
2. Tripping.
3. Jumping in (against the player with the ball) with both feet.
4. Charging an opponent in a dangerous or violent manner.
5. Charging from behind, unless the opponent is obstructing.
6. Striking or attempting to strike an opponent.
7. Holding.
8. Pushing.
9. Intentionally carrying, striking, or propelling the ball with hand or arm. The key word here is "intentionally," and the referee decides whether the hand ball was accidental or not—a decision that causes much contention and frustration in soccer.

The direct free kick is taken at the point of occurrence unless

1. An offensive player intentionally commits the infraction in the defensive penalty box, in which case the kick is taken from anywhere in that half of the penalty box. (All offensive players must be out of the box, and the ball must be kicked outside the box before it may be touched again by another offensive player.)
2. The player of the defensive team intentionally commits the infraction in the defensive penalty box, for which a penalty kick is awarded.

The *penalty kick* is taken twelve yards from the center of the goalpost, on a premarked spot. All players except for the goalkeeper and kicker must be outside the penalty box. The goalkeeper must remain with feet touching the goal line until the kick is taken and may not move sooner, or the kick may be retaken. The kicker may not touch the ball again unless it first strikes or is touched by another player of either team. Should the ball hit a goalpost or crossbar and rebound to the kicker, it may not be touched or the defensive team is awarded an indirect free kick.

An *indirect free kick* is awarded for the following six offenses:

1. Playing in a manner considered dangerous (i.e., attempting to kick the ball while it is being held by the goalkeeper).
2. Charging an opponent while the ball is not within playing distance of the players concerned.
3. Intentionally obstructing an opponent while not playing the ball (i.e., running between the opponent and the ball, or interposing the body between the opponent and the ball).
4. Charging the goalkeeper.
5. The goalkeeper is taking more than three steps while holding or bouncing the ball, or catching the ball and dropping it to the ground, then picking it up again.
6. Delaying the game or using tactics to waste time (i.e., kicking the ball away to slow down the other team's throw-in, or taking too long to make your own throw-in). In some cases, a coach who intentionally wastes time by making frequent substitutions may also be declared in violation and given a yellow card caution.

Caution with a *yellow card* is given if the player

1. Is deemed to be persistently infringing on the rules.
2. Shows dissent with the referee by word or action.
3. Is guilty of unsportsmanlike conduct.
4. Enters or leaves the field without the referee's consent.

In addition to the caution, an indirect free kick is awarded to the opposing team at the point of the infraction.

A *red card* and ejection is given if the player

1. Is guilty of violent conduct or serious foul play.
2. Uses foul or abusive language.
3. Persists in misconduct after being cautioned.

Free Kicks

Free kicks are divided into two categories: *direct* and *indirect*.

Direct kicks may be shot right into the goal for a score. Indirect kicks must first touch another player after being taken before they can count as a goal. If an indirect kick is shot into the goal, a free kick is awarded to the defending team.

When a free kick is being taken, the players of the opposing team must be at least ten yards away from the ball until it is kicked. Any violation of this rule results in the kick being retaken. This is at the discretion of the referee, who may allow a goal to be scored from the kick rather than call the infraction.

When a player is taking a free kick inside his own penalty area, all opposing players must remain outside the penalty area and at least ten yards from the ball. The ball is in play only after it has crossed the penalty box line.

The only time the defensive players may be closer than ten yards to the ball on a free kick is when they are inside their own penalty box, at which time they must be at least half the distance to the goal line if the ball is placed less than ten yards from the goal line.

The ball must be stationary when a free kick is taken. The kicker may not play the ball a second time until it has touched or been played by another player.

Throw-ins

The ball is thrown in at the point where it went out-of-bounds. (The entire ball must go over the sideline for it to be out.)

The thrower must face the field, and part of each foot must be on the sideline or on the ground outside the sideline. The thrower must use both hands and deliver the ball from behind and over the head. (See Chapter 9.)

The thrower must not touch the ball again until it is first touched by another player. A goal may not be scored directly from a throw-in.

If the ball is improperly thrown, it is given over to the other team to throw. If the thrower plays the ball a second time before it has been touched by another player, a free kick is awarded to the opposing team.

The Goal Kick

The goal kick is awarded to the defensive team when the offensive team last touches the ball before it goes over the goal line outside the goalposts. The kick is taken at that side of the small goal area immediately in front of the goalmouth.

The ball must go out of the penalty area before another player may touch it. Opposing players must remain outside the penalty box while the kick is taken.

If the kicker touches the ball a second time before it is touched by another player, an indirect free kick is awarded the opposing team.

The Corner Kick

When the ball crosses the goal line outside the goalposts, and is last touched by the defensive team, a corner kick is awarded to the opposing team.

This kick is a direct kick and is taken from the corner of the field at the side of the goal where the ball went out-of-bounds. The ball must be placed in the quarter circle inscribed at the corner.

Defensive players must be at least ten yards away from the kick. Other direct-kick rules apply.

Offensive players are not offsides when a corner kick is taken until the moment an offensive player touches the ball.

The Advantage Rule

The advantage rule is not a rule per se, but a convention of soccer throughout the world: If the referee judges an offensive player to have an advantage after being fouled, then play is allowed to continue.

The referee should not stop play for a defensive foul if by stopping play the offensive team is in effect penalized and loses any advantage it may have gained. Good referees sometimes delay their whistle momentarily to determine whether the offensive player does indeed have an advantage.

Referees in the United States often call out, "Play on!" indicating that the defensive infraction has been seen, but "advantage" belongs to the attacker.

Key Rules to Understand

- Free kicks require defenders to be at least ten yards from the ball, and the kicker may not touch the ball again until another player touches it.
- A kicker taking a penalty may not touch the ball if it rebounds off a goalpost or crossbar until it is touched by another player.
- Offsides is a judgment call by the referee, who decides whether the player's team gains advantage from an offsides position.
- A player cannot be offsides on corner kicks, goal kicks, or throw-ins.
- Technically, a hand ball must be intentional, and the referee might not call it if it is deemed accidental; of course, in the penalty box, most referees are inclined to call the hand ball and award a penalty. What matters here is consistency on the part of the official.
- A player taking a throw-in must have both feet on the ground and be facing the field at the moment of delivery.

SOCCER ORGANIZATIONS

As with those of all countries, U.S. soccer leagues are affiliated with a national organization. The United States Soccer Federation (USSF) is in turn a member of the Fédération Internationale de Football Association (FIFA), which sets rules and policies that control player status and club regulations, as well as organizes all international play, such as the World Cup tournament.

Below are the addresses of FIFA and the USSF along with the leading American soccer organizations that are affiliated with them.

Fédération Internationale de Football Association (FIFA)
P.O. Box 85
8030 Zurich, Switzerland

U.S. Soccer Federation (USSF)
U.S. Soccer House
1801–1811 S. Prairie Avenue
Chicago, IL 60616

U.S. World Cup Headquarters
2049 Century Park East, Suite 4400
Los Angeles, CA 90067

U.S. Youth Soccer Association, Inc.
Campbell Business Center
2050 N. Piano Road, Suite 100
Richardson, TX 75082

American Youth Soccer Organization (AYSO)
5403 W. 138th Street
Hawthorne, CA 90250

Soccer Association for Youth (SAY)
4903 Vine Street
Cincinnati, OH 45217

National Soccer Coaches Association of America
4220 Shawnee Mission Parkway, Suite 105B
Fairway, KS 66205

U.S. Amateur Soccer Association
7800 River Road
North Bergen, NJ 07047

Amateur Athletic Union
AAU House
3400 W. 86th Street
P.O. Box 68207
Indianapolis, IN 46268

National Collegiate Athletic Association (NCAA)
6201 College Boulevard
Overland Park, KS 66211–2422

Intercollegiate Soccer Association of America (ISAA)
Cornell University
Box 729
Ithaca, NY 14851

National Association of Intercollegiate Athletics (NAIA)
1221 Baltimore Avenue
Kansas City, MO 64105

National Federation Interscholastic Coaches and Officials
Association
11724 Plaza Circle
P.O. Box 20626
Kansas City, MO 64195

The National Soccer Hall of Fame

The Hall of Fame was originally founded by the Philadelphia Old-Timers Association to identify and honor those who have contributed to U.S. soccer.

Between 1950 and 1953 the Philadelphia organization sponsored the effort to establish a Hall of Fame. At its thirty-seventh annual convention in 1953 the USSF formally accepted responsibility for the Hall of Fame's development.

In 1982 the National Soccer Hall of Fame museum was opened in Oneonta, New York, the result of a combined effort by USSF officials and the local soccer organization. The museum is chartered by the state Board of Regents. The Hall of Fame is also developing a complex

The National Soccer Hall of Fame in Oneonta, New York, exhibits artifacts, photographs, and ephemera documenting the history of soccer in America since Colonial days. *Courtesy the National Soccer Hall of Fame at Oneonta, New York, Inc.*

of playing fields called the Wright National Soccer Campus, which was dedicated June 6, 1989.

The museum holdings include an extensive soccer memorabilia collection, including uniforms, trophies, films, photographs, and other archival material. One of the museum's showpieces is the ball used in America's now-famous 1–0 World Cup tournament victory over England in Brazil in 1950.

The Hall of Fame, which sponsors soccer tournaments and educational programs, is supported by membership, museum fees, and contributions.

National Soccer Hall of Fame
5-11 Ford Avenue
Oneonta, NY 13820-9924

BILL OF RIGHTS FOR YOUNG ATHLETES
(American Youth Soccer Organization)

Right of opportunity to participate in sports regardless of ability level.

Right to participate at a level that is commensurate with each child's developmental level.

Right to have qualified adult leadership.

Right to participate in safe and healthy environments.

Right to share in the leadership and decision-making of the sport.

Right to play as a child and not as an adult.

Right to proper preparation for participation in the sport.

Right to equal opportunity to strive for success.

Right to be treated with dignity by all involved.

Right to have fun through sport.

"Be a Good Sport"

(Excerpts from AYSO Sportsmanship Codes)

COACH'S CODE

Impress on your players that they must abide by the rules of the game at all times.

Develop team respect for the ability of opponents, as well as for the judgment of referees and opposing coaches.

Set a good example and be generous with your praise when it is deserved. Children need a coach they can respect.

PARENT'S CODE

Do not force an unwilling child to participate in sports.

Do not ridicule or yell at your child for making a mistake or for losing a game.

Applaud good plays by your team and by members of the opposing team.

Do not publicly question the referee's judgment and never his honesty.

Recognize the importance of volunteer coaches, referees, and officials and give them due respect. Without them there would be no AYSO.

Support all efforts to remove verbal and physical abuse from youth sporting activities.

PLAYER'S CODE

Play for the fun of it, not just to please your parents or coach.

Never argue with or complain about the referee's calls or decisions.

Control your temper, and most of all, resist the temptation to retaliate when you feel you have been wronged.

Concentrate on playing soccer and on affecting the outcome of the game with your best effort. Work equally as hard for your team as for yourself.

Be a good sport by cheering all good plays, whether it is your team's or your opponent's.

Treat all players as you would like to be treated. Remember that the goals of the game are to have fun, improve your skills, and feel good. Don't be a show-off or a ball hog.

A "Be a Good Sport" patch is given by AYSO regions to honor members who stand out when it comes to sportsmanship.

THE CARE OF INJURIES

While serious injuries should be cared for promptly by a physician, soccer players should become familiar with basic first aid in order to care for the minor injuries that occur regularly. The following is not intended to take the place of adequate medical supervision.

Overview/Approach

The first rule of thumb is to remain as relaxed as possible, especially if it is someone else who is hurt and you are coming to render assistance.

If you are the injured person, try to stay calm and breathe naturally. Do not try to get up or sit up until a coach or knowledgeable parent arrives to examine you.

Do not allow frightened persons to rattle you. Remember, injuries often seem worse at first than they really are, especially if there is some bleeding. On the other hand, a seemingly minor injury such as a backache could be serious if you keep on playing.

Playing with Pain/Playing While Hurt

While it is common for the athlete to play with some pain, no one should play or practice with a serious injury.

Obviously serious conditions—fractures, open wounds, torn muscles, heat exhaustion—as well as less obvious ones should be examined by a coach, parent, or physician to determine the care required. Among the more minor problems are sprained ankles, blisters, and scrapes or burns from sliding. Sprains must be given a chance to heal. Blisters, scrapes, and burns must be cleared up before they become infected.

While playing with occasional minor pain is part of the athlete's self-discipline, learning how to deal safely with that pain and heal that minor injury is also an important part of the young athlete's learning experience.

For instance, proper taping can permit a player to compete with a minor sprained ankle, but the athlete must do everything possible, including rest, to allow the injury to heal completely.

Common Injuries and First Aid

ABRASIONS AND SKIN BURNS: These surface injuries to skin caused by sliding must be cared for immediately. They are not only painful, but can become infected. Wash with first aid cleansing solution and cover with gauze. Later, clean with plain unperfumed soap twice a day, making sure to eliminate all dirt and foreign material.

Keep the wound exposed to promote drying and healing.

MINOR BACK PAIN: If you strain the muscles of your back, leave the field immediately and consult with your coach. Ice can help keep swelling down, but do not apply ice to your spine. In time, a combination of rest, hot baths, and liniment can cure a minor back injury.

Before playing again, be sure to warm up and stretch. Do not attempt full-scale match play until your back muscles are strong again. Recurring back pain can sideline you for a long time.

SEVERE BACK PAIN: If the pain is serious, or if there is weakness or numbness in your legs, you must see a physician, and you may require an ambulance. You should not be moved without a stretcher.

BLISTERS: Blisters are the accumulation of fluid between layers of the skin as a result of friction caused perhaps by shoes that are too small, socks that have become wrinkled, or new shoes to which your feet are not accustomed.

If the blister is unbroken, use a sterile needle to make a small hole and gently push out the fluid. Leave the skin over the blister as a protective covering and place a Band-Aid over that.

If the blister is torn open, cut away the skin with sterile scissors, then soak your foot in warm, soapy water. Apply antibiotic ointment and keep the wound covered with a sterile dressing or large Band-Aid. Drugstores can provide protective dressings or plasters to help the blister heal.

Until the blister is fully healed, be sure to keep it covered with a Band-Aid at all times. Every time the blister is injured, healing is delayed.

Whenever you play after a long layoff, or with new soccer shoes, watch for the first sign of blisters. Sometimes a very thin pair of socks worn under regular soccer socks can ease the friction of new shoes.

BRUISES: Caused by blows to the body, bruises can last several weeks, especially if the injured area is a bone. Immediately elevate the injured area and apply ice and compress with elastic wrap to prevent further swelling. Later, take regular hot baths. One favored remedy is to soak the area in a solution of Epsom salts and hot water; doing this helps relieve the pain.

HEAT STRESS: This can be dangerous if not attended to immediately. Heat stress is classified in four ways:

1. *Heat cramps* result from depletion of sodium through excessive sweating along with exercise that requires forceful, repetitive muscle contraction. These cramps are most common in the abdomen and calves.

Treatment includes rehydration with an electrolyte drink and/or water, and rest in a cool spot. As a preventive measure, increase your table salt intake at meals and eat foods rich in potassium.

2. *Heat syncope (fainting)* is caused by lack of oxygen to the brain as a result of dilation of blood vessels as the body tries to cool itself.

General body weakness, a grayish skin tone, severe fatigue, blurred vision, and elevated temperature are symptoms. As treatment, lie down in a cool place with your legs elevated, and take in small amounts of salt solution.

3. *Heat exhaustion* is caused by prolonged sweating without adequate fluid or electrolyte replacement.

Symptoms are profuse sweating, headache, nausea/vomiting, dizziness, undue fatigue, loss of coordination, mental confusion, rapid but strong pulse, and increased skin/body temperature.

Rest in a cool spot with your legs elevated, and remove excess clothing to increase the surface area exposed to air. Decrease your body temperature with iced towels and by getting out of the sun. Hydrate with water, salt solution, or an electrolyte drink. If improvement is not immediate, see a physician.

4. *Heat stroke* is a medical emergency, a failure of the body's ability to regulate its temperature.

Symptoms include hot and dry skin with no sweating, extremely high body temperature (104°–106° F), irrational behavior, loss of coordination, vomiting, rapid and shallow respiration, a rapid and weak pulse, seizure, unconsciousness, and coma. (Symptoms do not have to occur in this sequence.)

To treat, remove excess clothing and immediately decrease the body temperature with iced towels, shade, or whatever is available. Contact emergency medical services, treat for shock, and transport to a hospital.

MUSCLE CRAMPS: Overstress of muscles can happen even to athletes in top condition. Stretch the muscle until the pain is gone. If the pain is in your calf, push your foot against a hard, resistant surface until the pain subsides. If the cramp is in the right side of your abdomen, reach up as high as you can with your right hand until the pain is gone. Do the same for your left.

Use ice on the muscle if the pain does not go away.

NECK INJURY: If the pain is severe or if there is numbness or lack of sensation, do not attempt to move. Send for an ambulance. What seems to be a head injury might actually be a neck injury.

NOSEBLEED: Sit down and apply cold cloths or ice to your nose while applying pressure by pinching the bridge of your nose on the same side as your bleeding nostril. If the bleeding or pain persists, consult a physician immediately.

SPRAINED ANKLE: Apply ice immediately, elevate your foot, and bind with elastic wrap. In the case of severe pain or swelling, consult a physician. Stay off your foot until the pain has gone. Again, soaking in a solution of Epsom salts and hot water can do much to alleviate discomfort and promote proper circulation.

STRAINED MUSCLES: Pulls or tears to muscles should be treated with ice, your injured limb elevated and compressed with elastic wrap. Rest and gradual rehabilitation are essential to prevent a recurrence of the injury, which often occurs when you fail to warm up and stretch properly.

TOOTH INJURY: In the case of tooth breakage or loss, the tooth should be recovered and wrapped in a wet cloth so it can be transported with you to the doctor or dentist in the possibility it can be saved.

TRAUMA TO TESTICLES: If you are already on the ground, remain there, on your back, legs bent, and feet on the ground; otherwise, assume this position. Breathe slowly, inhaling through your nose and exhaling through your mouth.

One old method that often works is to have someone stand straddling you and then reach down with both hands and lift you gently from your hips. Having someone lift your hips and lower back off the ground and then carefully lower them again several times can help relieve the discomfort. (Make sure your teammates gather round to give you some privacy.)

If the pain persists, or if there is swelling in the scrotum or one testicle appears to have been displaced, then this is an emergency that must be appropriately cared for by a physician.

WINDED, OR WIND KNOCKED OUT: Relax and, when you can, breathe methodically through your nose and mouth. When you can stand up, raise both arms above your head, then slowly bend and touch your toes. Repeat this several times to replenish oxygen.

GLOSSARY

Association Football   The formal international name for soccer.

Ball hog   A player who dribbles selfishly. It's a term sometimes wrongly applied by some youth coaches to all players who dribble when the coach wants them to pass (especially to the coach's own kid).

Bend   A British term meaning to kick a ball hard, with spin that makes it curve.

Bicycle kick   An acrobatic overhead kick, taken by the player going for a ball above his head and kicking it backward.

Center circle   The marked ten-yard-radius circle in the center of the field from which the kickoff is taken.

Centering   Crossing the ball from the right or left side of the field into the middle, usually into the penalty area.

Changing the field   Crossing the ball with a long pass from the crowded side of the field to the other, more open side. Sometimes it's called for on the field with "Change it!"

Charging   A defensive effort to get the ball by leaning into the attacker with the shoulder. It's an effective move when done legally, meeting the opponent's weight with your own; it's a foul when you lean in too far and ram the opponent off balance.

Chip   Lifting the ball with a short pass over the defense.

Corner kick   An offensive free kick taken from the corner after the ball has been knocked over the goal line (not into the goal) by a defender. Attackers cannot be offsides on a corner.

Cross   To play the ball, usually in the air, from one side of the field into the middle or to the other side.

Crossbar   The horizontal section of the goalposts, twenty-four feet long in regular goals.

Dangerous play   An infraction in which a player is put at risk of injury. It usually involves taking a high kick while close to another player or lowering your own head to get a ball that is being kicked normally.

Dead ball   1. A ball that must be put into play with a free kick (restart) because the referee has whistled for stoppage in play or the ball has gone over the goal (end) line. 2. A ball that is not moving when the player kicks it.

Direct kick   A kick from a dead ball position. It may be shot directly into the goal to score.

Dribbling   Moving the ball with short kicks while keeping it under control in order to get away from defenders or to break through defenders for a shot at goal or to make a pass.

Drop ball   The way a referee puts a ball into play after a temporary stoppage. A player from each team stands in a face-off and the referee drops the ball between them. The ball must strike the ground before it can be played.

Far post   The defenders' goalpost farthest away from the attacker with the ball.

FIFA   Fédération Internationale de Football Association, organized soccer's international governing body, headquartered in Zurich, Switzerland, and sponsors of the World Cup.

First-timing   Kicking the ball without trapping it first.

Flick pass   A short, deceptive pass made quickly with the outside of your foot.

Football   1. A ball game played on foot rather than on horseback. 2. The term for soccer used by Americans with inferiority complexes.

Free kick The kick taken to restart play after an infraction, a score, or the ball going over a goal line for a corner or goal kick. Free kicks are either "direct," meaning the kick can score without the ball having to be touched by another player from either team, or "indirect," in which the ball must first be touched by another player to count.

Goalkeeper (goalie, keeper) This player defends the goal and may use his hands when inside the penalty box.

Goal kick A restart kick, taken by the defensive team after the ball is last played over the goal line (not into the goal) by the attacking team.

Goalmouth The area right in front of the goal.

Half volley A kick taken at the moment the ball bounces.

Hand ball An infraction caused when a field player touches the ball with his hand or arm.

Hat trick One player scoring three goals in a game. Some interpretations state that the three goals must be scored consecutively.

Heading Striking or guiding the ball with your head, preferably with your forehead.

Indirect kick A kick from a dead ball position. The ball must be touched by another player (offense or defense) before it can count as a score.

Instep kick A straight-ahead kick taken with the top of your foot. It is a particularly powerful and accurate kick.

Inswinger A corner kick into the air that curves toward the goalmouth.

International 1. An all-star player who represents his country's national team in matches against other national teams. 2. A match between national teams.

Kickoff The first kick taken at the center of the field to begin the game or to restart play after a goal has been scored. The ball must travel forward and go its full circumference before it can be touched by the next player.

Linesman   One of two subordinate officials in the single-referee format; runs along the sidelines and signals with a flag when the ball goes out-of-bounds. Linesmen indicate which team takes possession and signal infractions and offsides. The referee judges whether to stop play when the linesman waves a flag, and in many cases the linesman is consulted in situations when the referee is not certain of what happened.

Long pass   Unstoppable and very exciting when done right, it is usually given backspin and curve to make it float just over the defense and then die rather than roll away when it lands.

Marking   Covering an attacker closely.

Near post   The defenders' goalpost closest to the attacker with the ball.

Obstruction   An infraction in which the player who has the ball blocks the opponent from getting to it but does not attempt to play the ball.

Offsides   An infraction called on an attacking player in the offensive half of the field if, at the instant the ball is played by a teammate, there are not at least two defenders between the player and the goal. If the ball is ahead of the player at the moment it is played, the player is not offsides.

Off the ball   Running without the ball in possession, looking to get open for a pass.

Outswinger   A corner kick in the air that curves away from the goalmouth.

Overlapping   When a midfielder or fullback runs forward outside the wings to receive a pass and go momentarily on the attack.

Own-goal   A goal scored against a team by its own player.

Penalty   A direct free kick taken from a spot twelve yards in front of the goal, with only the goalie permitted to stop the ball and all players required to stay outside the penalty area.

Penalty area   The box in front of the goal in which the goalie may use his hands to catch or block the ball. This box is thirty-six yards wide and sixteen yards deep on a regular soccer field.

Pitch   A British term for the field.

Red card   A signal for ejection, usually issued after an earlier yellow card warning has first been given. The red card is held up by the referee to signal a player's or coach's ejection from the game. The player's number is taken, and league officials decide on further punishment, such as fines and/or suspension.

Referee   The official (or in scholastic soccer, one of two officials) who runs the game on the field, keeping the time and controlling play. The single referee, although assisted by linesmen, is the final authority in rules interpretation.

Rover   A player with mainly offensive responsibilities who is free to move around the field as the play requires. He can also come back on defense if need be.

Save   When the goalkeeper prevents the ball from going into the net. A save is not counted every time a goalie handles the ball, but only when there is a threat of a goal being scored.

Screening   Shielding the ball with your body, staying between the defender and the ball and preventing a defender from getting a kick at it.

Short pass   An effective way for a team to keep possession of the ball.

Side-foot kick   Not the only way to kick a soccer ball; used usually for short passes.

Sliding tackle   A defensive move, usually done in desperation, in which the player slides at the ball as it is being dribbled by the offensive player, in an attempt to knock the ball away.

Soccer   The American name for Association Football.

Spot kick   A British term for penalty kick.

Square pass   A short or medium pass pushed perpendicularly to the direction of play to an open teammate. It is usually called for on the field with "Square!"

Stopper   In certain defensive formations, the player called upon to block and repel the attack in the center of the field, often as the last defender.

Striker   An offensive player whose main task is to stay up front and receive passes, with the aim of taking the most direct route to the goal.

Sweeper, libero   A defensive player who is at liberty to play as needed in response to the opponent's attack, and without a specific opponent to mark. He is the last player on defense.

Tackling   Attempting to get the ball from an attacker by blocking the ball with your feet and legs.

Through pass   A pass played between defensive players or over their heads to an open space where an attacker can run for it.

Throw-in   When the ball is thrown back into play by one team after being knocked out-of-bounds by the other team. A goal may not be scored directly from a throw-in.

Toe ball   A very good way to kick sometimes, especially when taking a close shot.

Touchline   A British term meaning "sidelines." "Out-of-touch" means the ball is out-of-bounds over the sideline.

Trapping   The act of stopping and controlling a ball.

USSF   United States Soccer Federation, the governing body of organized soccer in this country, subordinate to FIFA.

Wall   The lining up of several defenders to block a free kick that is taken close enough to their goal to be dangerous.

Wall pass   Two players bypassing a defender by quickly passing to each other, the receiving player acting much like a wall by letting the pass bounce off his foot, directing it into the path of the passer, who is running behind the defender.

World Cup   Officially the Jules Rimet Trophy, named after the Frenchman who founded it, this international tournament is played every four years by the national teams of almost 150 countries, which compete in regional competition until 22 finalists join the previous cup's winner and the host country's national team for the final tournament.

Yellow card   A card held up to signal a warning for a flagrant, serious infraction. The yellow card is shown to the players and coaches by the referee, who writes down the number of the perpetrator. A second yellow card results in the player being ejected from the game.

SELECTED BIBLIOGRAPHY AND SUGGESTED READING

Bradley, Gordon, and Clive Toye. *Playing Soccer the Professional Way.* New York: Harper & Row, 1973.

Caruso, Andrew. *Soccer Coaching Ages 5–12.* Quakertown, Penn.: Soccer Coaching Press, 1992.

————. *Soccer Coaching, the Great Game.* Quakertown, Penn.: Soccer Coaching Press, 1989.

Foulds, Sam, and Paul Harris. *America's Soccer Heritage.* Manhattan Beach, Cal.: Soccer for Americans, 1979.

Hollander, Zander. *The American Encyclopedia of Soccer.* New York: Everest House Publishers, 1980.

Kane, Basil G. *Soccer for American Spectators.* South Brunswick and New York: A.S. Barnes and Co., 1970.

Lauffer, Robert. *Coaching Soccer.* New York: Sterling Publishing, 1989.

Pelé (Edson Arantes do Nascimento) with Robert Fish. *My Life and the Beautiful Game.* New York: Warner Books, 1977.

Rote, Kyle, Jr., with Basil Kane. *The Complete Book of Soccer.* New York: Simon & Schuster, 1978.

Schellscheidt, Manny. *Youth League Soccer Skills.* North Palm Beach, Fla.: The Athletic Institute, 1989.

Vogelsinger, Hubert. *The Challenge of Soccer.* 2nd ed. LaJolla, Cal.: Inswinger, Inc., 1982.

INDEX

ABOUT THE AUTHOR

Stuart Murray is a former college and semi-pro soccer player who has coached youngsters since 1974, including high school, club, and recreation league soccer.

The father of four soccer-playing children, Murray is the author of four works of nonfiction and nine novels; he has been a newspaper reporter and columnist, editor of regional and trade magazines, and a book editor.

Murray was born in Scotland, where he first learned to kick a ball for the fun of it. When he was eight, he came to the United States, later playing high school soccer in Irvington, New Jersey, and then with athletes from more than twenty nations in the German-American League, the American League, and at Rutgers University.

Murray is a member of the National Soccer Coaches Association of America and is a member of the American Soccer History and Research Committee for the United States Soccer Federation.